GRAND STREET

36

Grand Street is set in New Caledonia by TEXSource, Houston, Tex., and printed by W. E. Barnett & Associates, Houston, Tex. Color separations and halftones are by Color Separations, Inc., Houston, Tex.

Cover: Saul Steinberg, untitled (detail), 1964.

Elizabeth Bishop's "Was It in His Hand?" is courtesy of Vassar College Library.

Grand Street (ISSN 0734-5496; ISBN 36-0-393-30740-9) is published quarterly by Grand Street Press (a project of the New York Foundation for the Arts, Inc., a not-for-profit corporation), 135 Central Park West, New York, N.Y. 10023. Contributions and gifts to Grand Street Press, a project of the New York Foundation for the Arts, Inc., are tax-deductible to the extent allowed by law.

Unsolicited material should be addressed to the editors at *Grand Street,* 135 Central Park West, New York, N.Y. 10023. Manuscripts will not be returned unless accompanied by a stamped, self-addressed envelope.

Second-class postage at New York, N.Y., and additional mailing offices. Postmaster: Please send address changes to *Grand Street,* 305 Main Street, Westport, Conn. 06880.

Subscription orders and address changes should be addressed to *Grand Street,* 305 Main Street, Westport, Conn. 06880. Subscriptions are $24 a year (four issues). Foreign subscriptions (including Canada) are $34 a year, and must be payable in U.S. funds. Single-copy price is $8.50. *Grand Street* is distributed by W. W. Norton & Company, 500 Fifth Avenue, New York, N.Y. 10110.

CONTENTS

Little Miracles, Kept Promises

Ex-Voto Donated as Promised

On the 20th of December of 1988 we suffered a terrible disaster on the road to Corpus Christi. The bus we were riding skidded and overturned near Robstown and a lady and her little girl were killed. Thanks to la Virgen de Guadalupe we are alive, all of us miraculously unharmed, and with no visible scars, except we are afraid to ride buses. We dedicate this retablo to la Virgencita with our affection and gratitude and our everlasting faith.

Familia Arteaga
Alice, Texas
G.R.(Gracias Recibido/Thanks Given)

Blessed Santo Niño de Atocha,

Thank you for helping us when Chapa's truck got stolen. We didn't know how we was going to make it. He needs it to get to work, and this job, well, he's been on probation since we got him to quit drinking. Raquel and the kids are hardly ever afraid of him anymore, and we are proud parents. We don't know how we can repay you for everything you have done for our family.

We will light a candle to you every Sunday and never forget you.

Sidronio Tijerina
Brenda A. Camacho de Tijerina
San Angelo, Texas

Dear San Martín de Porres,

Please send us clothes, furniture, shoes, dishes. We need anything that don't eat. Since the fire we have to start all over again and Lalo's disability check ain't much and don't go far. Zulema would like to finish school but I says she can just forget about it now. She's our oldest and her place is at home helping us out I told her. Please make her see some sense. She's all we got.

Thanking you,
Adelfa Vásquez
Escobas, Texas

Dear San Antonio de Padua,

Can you please help me find a man who isn't a pain in the nalgas. There aren't any in Texas, I swear. Especially not in San Antonio.

Can you do something about all the educated Chicanos who have to go to California to find a job. I guess what my sister Irma says is true, "If you didn't get a husband when you were in college, you don't get one."

I would appreciate it very much if you sent a man who speaks Spanish, who at least can pronounce his name the way it's supposed to be pronounced. Someone please who never calls himself "Hispanic" unless he's applying for a grant from Washington, D.C.

Can you send me a man man. I mean someone who's not ashamed to be seen cooking, or cleaning, or looking after himself. In other words, a man who acts like an adult. Not one who's never lived alone, never bought his own underwear, never ironed his own shirts, never even heated his own tortillas. In other words, don't send me someone like my brothers, who my mother ruined with too much chichi, or I'll throw him back.

I'll turn your statue upside down until you send him to me. I've put up with too much too long, and now I'm just too intelligent, too powerful, too beautiful, too sure of who I am finally to deserve anything less.

Ms. Barbara Ybañez
San Antonio, TX

Dear Niño Fidencio,

I would like for you to help me get a job with good pay, benefits, and retirement plan. I promise you if you help me I will make a pilgrimage to your tomb in Espinazo and bring you flowers. Many thanks.

César Escandón
Pharr, Tejas

DEAR DON PEDRITO JARAMILLO HEALER OF LOS OLMOS

MY NAME IS ENRIQUETA ANTONIA SANDOVAL I LIVE IN SAN MARCOS TX I AM SICK THEY OPERATED ME FROM A KIDNEY AND A TUMOR OF CANCER BUT THANKS TO GOD I AM ALIVE BUT I HAVE TO GET TREATMENTS FOR A YEAR THE KIMO I AM 2½ YEARS OLD BUT MY GRANDMA BROUGHT ME THAT YOU AND OUR LORD WHO IS IN THE HEAVENS WILL CURE ME WITH THIS LETTER THAT I AM DEPOSITING HERE ITS MY GRANDMA WHO IS WRITING THIS I HOPE EVERYBODY WHO SEES THIS LETTER WILL TAKE A MINUTE TO ASK FOR MY HEALTH

ENRIQUETA ANTONIA SANDOVAL
2 AND A HALF YEARS OLD

I LEOCADIA DIMAS VDA. DE CORDERO OF SAN MARCOS TX HAVE COME TO PAY THIS REQUEST TO DON PEDRITO THAT MY GRANDDAUGHTER WILL COME OUT FINE FROM HER OPERATION THANKS TO GOD AND THOSE WHO HELPED SUCH GOOD DOCTORS THAT DID THEIR JOB WELL THE REST IS IN GODS HANDS THAT HE DO HIS WILL MANY THANKS WITH ALL MY HEART

YOUR VERY RESPECTFUL SERVANT
LEOCADIA

Oh Mighty Poderosos, Blessed "Powerful Ones,"

You who are crowned in heaven and who are so close to our Divine Savior, I implore your intercession before the Almighty on my behalf. I ask for peace of spirit and prosperity, and that the demons in my path that are the cause of all my woes be removed so that they no longer torment me. Look favorably on this petition and bless me, that I may continue to glorify your deeds with all my heart—Santísimo Niño Fidencio, Gran General Pancho Villa, Bendito Don Pedrito Jaramillo, Virtuoso John F. Kennedy, and Blessed Pope John Paul. Amen.

Gertrudis Parra
Uvalde, Tejas

Father Almighty,

Teach me to love my husband again. Forgive me.

s.
Corpus Christi

Seven African Powers that surround our Savior—Obatalia, Yemalia, Ochum, Orula, Ogum, Elegua, and Olofi—why don't you behave and be good to me? Oh Seven African Powers, come on, don't be bad. Let my Illinois lottery ticket win, and if it does, don't let my cousin Cirilo in Chicago cheat me out of my winnings, since I'm the one who pays for the ticket and all he does is buy it for me each week—if he does even that. He's my cousin, but like the bible says, better to say nothing than to say nothing nice.

Protect me from the evil eye of the envious and don't let my enemies do me harm, because I've never done a thing wrong to anyone first. Save this good Christian who the wicked have taken advantage of.

Seven Powers, reward my devotion with good luck. Look after me, why don't you? And don't forget me because I never forget you.

Moises Ildefonso Mata
San Antonio, Texas

Virgencita de Guadalupe,

I promise to walk to your shrine on my knees the very first day I get back, I swear, if you will only get the Tortilleria La Casa de la Masa to pay me the $253.72 they owe me for two weeks work. I put in 67½ hours that first week and 79 hours the second, and I don't have anything to show for it yet. I calculated with the taxes deducted, I have $253.72 coming to me. That's all I'm asking for. The $253.72 I have coming to me.

I have asked the proprietors Blanquita and Rudy Mondragón, and they keep telling me next week, next week, next week. And it's almost the middle of the third week already and I don't know how I'm going to do it to pay this week's rent, since I'm already behind, and the other guys have loaned me as much as they're able, and I don't know what I'm going to do, I don't know what I'm going to do.

My wife and the kids and my in-laws all depend on what I send home. We are humble people, Virgencita. You know I'm not full of vices. That's how I am. It's been hard for me to live here so far away without seeing my wife, you know. And sometimes one gets tempted, but no, and no, and no. I'm not like that. Please, Virgencita, all I'm asking for is my $253.72. There is no one else I can turn to here in this country, and well, if you can't help me, well, I just don't know.

Arnulfo Contreras
San Antonio, Tejas

Saint Sebastian, who was persecuted with arrows and then survived, thank you for answering my prayers! All them arrows that had persecuted me—my brother-in-law Ernie and my sister Alba and their kids—el Junior, la Gloria, and el Skyler—all gone. And now my home sweet home is mine again, and my Dianita bien lovey-dovey, and my kids got something to say to me besides who hit who.

Here is the little gold milagrito I promised you, a little house, see? And it ain't that cheap gold-plate shit either. So now that I paid you back, we're even, right? Cause I don't like for no one to say Victor Lozano don't pay his debts. I pays cash on the line, bro. And Victor Lozano's word like his deeds is solid gold.

Victor A. Lozano
Houston, TX

Dear San Lázaro,

My mother's comadre Demetria said if I prayed to you that like maybe you could help me because you were raised from the dead and did a lot of miracles and maybe if I lit a candle every night for seven days and prayed, you might maybe could help me with my face breaking out with so many pimples. Thank you.

Ruben Ledesma
Hebbronville, Texas

Santísma Señora de San Juan de los Lagos,

We came to see you twice when they brought you to San Antonio, my mother and my sister Yolanda and two of my aunts, tia Enedina and my tia Perla, and we drove all the way from Beeville just to visit you and make our requests.

I don't know what my tia Enedina asked for, she's always so secretive, but probably it had to do with her son Beto who doesn't do anything but hang around the house and get into trouble. And my tia Perla no doubt complained about her ladies' problems—her ovaries that itch, her tangled fallopians, her uterus that makes her seasick with all its flipping and flopping. And Mami, who said she only came along for the ride, lit three candles so you would bless us all and sweep jealousy and bitterness from our hearts because that's what she says every day and every night. And my sister Yoli asked that you help her lose weight because *I don't want to wind up like tia Perla, embroidering altar cloths and dressing saints.*

But that was a year ago, Virgencita, and since then my cousin Beto was fined for killing the neighbor's rooster with a flying Big Red bottle. And my tia Perla is convinced her uterus has fallen because when she walks something inside her rattles like a maraca. And my mother and my aunts are arguing and yelling at each other same as always. And my stupid sister Yoli is still sending away for even stupider products like the Grasa Fantastica, guaranteed to burn away fat—*It really works, Tere, just rub some on while you're watching t.v.*—only she's fatter than ever and just as sad.

What I realize is that we all made the trip to San Antonio to ask something of you, Virgencita, we all needed you to listen to us. And all of us, my mama and sister Yoli, and my aunts Enedina and Perla, of all of us, you granted me my petition and sent, just like I asked, a guy who would love only me because I was tired of looking at girls younger than me walking along the street, or riding in cars, or standing in front of the school with a guy's arm hooked around their neck.

So what is it I'm asking for? Please, Virgencita. Lift this heavy cross from my shoulders and leave me like I was before, wind on my neck, my arms swinging free, and no one telling me how I ought to be.

Teresa Galindo
Beeville, Texas

Miraculous Black Christ of Esquipulas,

Please make our grandson to be nice to us and stay away from drugs. Save him to find a job and move away from us. Thank you.

Grandma y Grandfather
Harlingen

M3rlc5l45s Bllck Chr3st 4f 2sq53p5lls,

3 lsk y45, L4rd, w3th 1ll my h21rt pl21s2 w1tch 4v2r M1nny B2n1v3d2s wh4 3s 4v2rs21s. 3 l4v2 h3m 1nd 3 d4n't kn4w wh1t t4 d4 1b45t 1ll th3s l4v2 s1dn2ss 1nd sh1m2 th1t f3lls m2.

B2nj1m3n T.
D2l R34 TX

Milagroso Cristo Negro de Esquipulas,

Te ofrezco este retrato de mis niños. Wáchelos, Dios Santo, y si le quitas el trago a mi hijo te prometo prender velitas. Ayúdanos con nuestras cuentas, Señor, y que el cheque del income tax nos llegue pronto para pagar los biles. Danos una buena vida y que les ayudes a mis hijos a cambiar sus modos. Tú que eres tan bondadoso escucha estas peticiones que te pido con todo mi corazón y con toda la fe de mi alma. Ten piedad, Padre mio. Mi nombre es **Adela O. Elizondo.**
Cotulla TX

Milagroso Cristo Negro,

Thank you por el milagro de haber graduado de high school. Aquí le regalo mi retrato de graduation.

Fito Moroles
Rockport, Texas

Cristo Negro,

Venimos desde muy lejos. Infinito gracias, Señor. Gracias por habernos escuchado.

Familia Armendáriz G.
Matamoros, Tamps. México

Jesus Christ,

Please keep Deborah Abrego and Ralph S. Urrea together forever.

Love,
Deborah Abrego
Sabinal, Texas

Blessed Virgen de los Remedios,

Señora Dolores Alcalá de Corchado finds herself gravely ill from a complication that resulted after a delicate operation she underwent Thursday last, and from which she was recovering satisfactorily until suffering a hemorrhage Tuesday morning. Please intercede on her behalf. We leave her in the hands of God, that his will be done, now that we have witnessed her suffering and don't know whether she should die or continue this life. Her husband of forty-eight years offers this request with all his heart.

Señor Gustavo Corchado B.
Laredo, Tejas

Madrecita de Dios,

Thank you. Our child is born healthy!

Rene y Janie Garza
Hondo, TX

Saint Jude, patron saint of lost causes,

Help me pass my English 320, British Restoration Literature class and everything to turn out ok.

Eliberto González
Dallas

• • •

Virgencita . . .

I've cut off my hair just like I promised I would and pinned my braid here by your statue. Above a Toys-R-Us nametag that says Izaura. Along several hospital bracelets. Next to a business card for Sergio's Casa de la Belleza Beauty College. Domingo Reyna's driver's license. Notes printed on the flap of envelopes. Silk roses, plastic roses, paper roses, roses crocheted out of fluorescent orange yarn. Photo button of a baby in a charro hat. Caramel-skinned woman in a white graduation cap and gown. Mean dude in bandanna and tattoos. Oval black and white passport portrait of the sad uncle who never married. A mama in a sleeveless dress watering the porch plants. Sweet boy with new mustache and new soldier uniform. Teenager with a little bit of herself sitting on her lap. Blurred husband and wife leaning one into the other as if joined at the hip. Black and white photo of the cousins la Josie y la Mary Helen, circa 1942. Polaroid of Sylvia Rios, First Holy Communion, age 9 years.

So many milagritos safety-pinned here, so many *little miracles* dangling from red thread—a gold Sacred Heart, a tiny copper arm, a kneeling man in silver, a bottle, a brass truck, a foot, a house, a hand, a baby, a cat, a breast, a tooth, a belly button, an evil eye. So many petitions, so many promises made and kept. And there is nothing I can give you except this braid of hair the color of coffee in a glass.

Chayo, what have you done! All that beautiful hair.

Chayito, how could you ruin in one second what your mother took years to create?

You might as well've plucked out your eyes like Saint Lucy. All that hair!

My mother cried, did I tell you? All that beautiful hair . . .

I've cut off my hair. Which I've never cut since the day I was born. The donkey tail in a birthday game. Something shed like a snakeskin.

My head as light as if I'd raised it from water. My heart buoyant again, as if before I'd worn the Corazon Sagrado in my open chest. I could've lit this entire church with my grief.

I'm a bell without a clapper. A woman with one foot in this world and one foot in that. A woman straddling both. This thing between my legs, this unmentionable.

I'm a snake swallowing its tail. I'm my history and my future. All my ancestors' ancestors inside my own belly. All my futures and all my pasts.

I've had to steel and hoard and hone myself. I've had to push the furniture against the door and not let you in.

What you doing sitting in there in the dark?

I'm thinking.

Thinking of what?

Just . . . thinking.

You're nuts. Chayo, ven a saludar. All the relatives are here. You come out of there and be sociable.

Do boys think, and girls daydream? Do only girls have to come out and greet the relatives and smile and be nice and quedar bien?

It's not good to spend so much time alone.

What she do in there by herself? It don't look right.

Chayito, when you getting married? Look at your cousin Leticia. She's younger than you.

How many kids you want when you grow up?

When I become a mommy . . .

You'll change. You'll see. Wait till you meet Mister Right.

Chayo, tell everybody what it is you're studying again.

Look at our Chayito. She likes making her little pictures. She's gonna be a painter.

A painter! Tell her I got five rooms that need painting.

When you become a mother . . .

Thank you for making all those months I held my breath not a child in my belly, but a thyroid problem in my throat.

I can't be a mother. Not now. Maybe never. Not for me to choose, like I didn't choose being female. Like I didn't choose being artist—it isn't something you choose. It's something you are, only I can't explain it.

I don't want to be a mother.

I wouldn't mind being a father. At least a father could still be artist, could love some thing instead of some one, and no one would call that selfish.

I leave my braid here and thank you for believing what I do is important. Though no one else in my family, no other woman, neither friend nor relative, no one I know, not even the heroine in the telenovelas, no woman wants to live alone.

I do.

Virgencita de Guadalupe. For a long time I wouldn't let you in my house. I couldn't see you without seeing my ma each time my father came home drunk and yelling, blaming everything that ever went wrong in his life on her.

I couldn't look at your folded hands without seeing my abuela mumbling, "My son, my son, my son . . ." Couldn't look at you without blaming you for all the pain my mother and her mother and all our mothers' mothers have put up with in the name of God. Couldn't let you in my house.

I wanted you bare-breasted, snakes in your hands. I wanted you leaping and somersaulting the backs of bulls. I wanted you swallowing raw hearts and rattling volcanic ash. I wasn't going to be my mother or my grandma. All that self-sacrifice, all that silent suffering. Hell no. Not here. Not me.

Don't think it was easy going without you. Don't think I didn't get my share of it from everyone. Heretic. Atheist. Malinchista. Hocicona. But I wouldn't shut my yap. My mouth always getting in trouble. Is *that* what they teach you at the university? Miss High-and-Mighty. Miss Thinks-She's-Too-Good-For-Us. Acting like a bolilla, a white girl. Malinche. Don't think it didn't hurt being called a traitor. Trying to explain to my ma, to my abuela why I didn't want to be like them.

I don't know how it all fell in place. How I finally understood who you are. No longer Mary the mild, but our mother Tonantzín. Your church at Tepeyac built on the site of her temple. Sacred ground no matter whose goddess claims it.

That you could have the power to rally a people when a country was born, and again during civil war, and during a farmworkers strike in California made me think maybe there is power in my mother's patience, strength in my grandmother's endurance. Because those who suffer have a special power, don't they? The power of understanding someone else's pain. And understanding is the beginning of healing.

When I learned your real name is Coatlaxopeuh, She Who Has Dominion Over Serpents, when I recognized you as Tonantzín, and learned your names are Teteoinnan, Toci, Xochiquetzal, Tlazolteotl, Coatlicue, Chalchiuhtlicue, Coyolxauhqui, Huixtocihuatl, Chicomecoatl, Cihuacoatl, when I could see you as Nuestra Señora de la Soledad, Nuestra Señora de los Remedios, Nuestra Señora del Perpetuo Socorro, Nuestra Señora de San Juan de los Lagos, Our Lady of Lourdes, Our Lady of Mount

Carmel, Our Lady of the Rosary, Our Lady of Sorrows, I wasn't ashamed, then, to be my mother's daughter, my grandmother's granddaughter, my ancestors' child.

When I could see you in all your facets, all at once the Buddha, the Tao, the true Messiah, Yahweh, Allah, the Heart of the Sky, the Heart of the Earth, the Lord of the Near and Far, the Spirit, the Light, the Universe, I could love you, and, finally, learn to love me.

• • •

Mighty Guadalupana Coatlaxopeuh Tonantzín,

What "little miracle" could I pin here? Braid of hair in its place and know that I thank you.

Rosario (Chayo) De Leon
Austin, Tejas

Alberto Giacometti

EDWARD SAID

On Jean Genet's Late Works

for Ben Sonnenberg

The first time I saw Jean Genet was in the spring of 1970, a theatrically turbulent and inchoate season when energies and ambitions were released from the social imagination of America into its social body. There was always some excitement to celebrate, some occasion to get up for, some new moment in the Indochinese war either to lament or demonstrate against. Just a couple of weeks before the American invasion of Cambodia, at what seemed the very height of the spring events at Columbia University—which, it should be recalled, had still not recovered from the upheavals of 1968: its administration feeling uncertain, its faculty badly divided, its students perpetually exercised both in and out of the classroom—a noon rally was announced in support of the Black Panthers. It was to take place on the steps of Low Library, Columbia's imposing administration building, and I was especially eager to attend because the rumor was that Jean Genet was going to speak. As I left Hamilton Hall for the rally, I met a student of mine who had been particularly active on campus and who assured me that Genet was indeed going to speak and that he, the student, would be Genet's simultaneous interpreter.

It was an unforgettable scene for two reasons. One was the

deeply moving sight of Genet himself, who stood at the center of a large crowd of Panthers and students—he was planted in the middle of the steps with his audience all around him rather than in front of him—dressed in his black leather jacket, blue shirt, and, I think, scruffy jeans. He seemed absolutely at rest, rather like the portrait of him by Giacometti, who catches the man's astounding combination of storminess, relentless control, and almost religious stillness. What I have never forgotten was the gaze of Genet's piercing blue eyes; they seemed to reach out across the distance and fix you with an enigmatic and curiously neutral look.

The other memorable aspect of that rally was the stark contrast between the declarative simplicity of Genet's French remarks in support of the Panthers, and the immensely baroque embellishment of them by my erstwhile student. Genet would say, for example, "The blacks are the most oppressed class in the United States." This would emerge in the translator's colorful ornamentation as something like "In this motherfucking son-of-a-bitch country, in which reactionary capitalism oppresses and fucks over all the people, not just some of them, etc. etc." Genet stood through this appalling tirade unruffled, and even though the tables were sufficiently turned that translator and not speaker dominated the proceedings, the great writer never so much as blinked. This added to my respect and interest in the man, who was swept away without a flourish at the end of his all-too-brief comments. Having known Genet's literary achievements through teaching *Notre-Dame des fleurs* and *The Thief's Journal,* I was surprised at what appeared from a distance to be his immaculate modesty, quite different from the violent and eccentric sentiments attributed to him by his translator, who allowed himself to ignore what Genet said during the rally in preference for the bordello and prison scatology of some of the plays and prose writings.

When I next saw Genet, it was in the late fall of 1972 in Beirut, where I was spending a sabbatical year. An old school friend of mine, Hanna (John) Mikhail, had called me some time before and said that he would like to bring Genet around to meet me, but I hadn't taken the offer very seriously at first, partly because I couldn't imagine Hanna and Genet as friends, and partly because I still knew nothing about Genet's already considerable involvement with the Palestinian resistance movement.

In any event, Hanna Mikhail deserves to be remembered seventeen years after the fact a little more substantially than I've just presented him. Hanna and I were exact contemporaries, he as a Palestinian undergraduate at Haverford in the mid-'50s, I at Princeton. We went to graduate school at Harvard at the same time, although he was in political science and Middle Eastern studies and I was in comparative literature and English. He was always an exceptionally decent, quiet, and intellectually brilliant man, who expressed to me a quite unique Palestinian Christian background, firmly rooted in the Quaker community of Ramallah. He was committed to Arab nationalism and, very much more than I, at home in both the Arab world and the West. I was flabbergasted when in 1969, after what I gathered was a difficult divorce from his American wife, he quit a good teaching position at the University of Washington and enlisted in the revolution, as we called it, which was headquartered in Amman. I met him there in 1969 and again in 1970 when, both before Black September and in its early days, he played a leading role as the head of information for Fateh.

Hanna's movement name was Abu Omar, and it is in that capacity and by that name that he appears in Genet's posthumous autobiographical work *Un Captif amoureux* (the English title, *Prisoner of Love*, misses much that is subtly interesting in the French original), which I think Genet considered to be a continuation of *The Thief's Journal*. Published in 1986, *Un Captif* is an astonishingly rich and rambling account of Genet's experiences with, feelings about, and reflections on the Palestinians, with whom he associated for about fifteen years. As I said, at the time of his visit I had no idea of Genet's already quite long involvement with the Palestinians, nor, in fact, did I know anything at all about his North African engagements, personal or political. Hanna had called at about eight that evening to say that they would both be dropping by a little later, and so after putting our infant son to bed, Mariam and I sat down to wait in the attractively warm and quiet Beirut evening.

I feel hesitant about reading too much into Genet's presence in that part of the world at that time, but in retrospect there is a correspondence between this unsettlingly brilliant *poète maudit* and much that has been bewildering and disturbing about recent events in Jordan, Palestine, and Lebanon. Genet was no ordinary visitor, no simple observer or Western traveler in search of exotic peoples and places to write up in some future book. Now, in recollection, his movements through Jordan and Lebanon had something like the effect of a seismographic reading, drawing and exposing the fault lines that a largely normal surface had hidden. I say this mainly because at the time I met him, 1972, although I had not read or seen *Les Paravents* (*The Screens*), his gigantic and iconoclastic drama about French colonialism and the Algerian resistance, and although *Un Captif amoureux* had not been written and would not appear for fourteen years, I sensed that this titanic personality had fully intuited the scope and drama of what we were living through, in Lebanon, Palestine, and elsewhere. The Lebanese Civil War would break out almost exactly three years later; Hanna would be killed four years later; the Israeli invasion of Lebanon would occur ten years later; and, very important indeed from my point of view, the *intifada* that would lead to the declaration of a Palestinian state was to explode into actuality fifteen years after. I could not have felt what I feel now, that the dislocating and yet rigorous energies and visions that informed *The Screens* would not, could not, be stilled after Algerian independence in 1962, but would, like the nomadic figures spoken of by Gilles Deleuze and Felix Guattari in *Mille plateaux*, wander elsewhere in search of acknowledgment and fulfillment.

In manner and appearance, Genet was as quiet and as modest as he had seemed at the Columbia rally. He and Hanna arrived a little after ten and stayed till almost three in the morning. I don't think I could narrate the meandering discussions of that evening, but I do want to register a few impressions and anecdotes. Hanna remained fairly quiet throughout; he later told me that he had wanted to let me feel the full force of Genet's vision of things without distraction. Later I was able to read back into that gesture some of the forgiving permission that Hanna had extended to everyone around him, and how that permission, that allowance for people to be themselves, was the true focus of

Hanna's search for liberation. Certainly it was clear that Genet appreciated this aspect of his companion's political mission; it was the deep bond between them, that both men in effect had united passion with an almost self-abnegating tolerance.

At the outset it seemed appropriate to tell Genet my spectator's side of the Panther rally and get his reaction to his interpreter's embellishments. He seemed unfazed: "I may not have said all those things," he said, "but," he added solemnly, "je les pensais." We talked about Sartre, whose enormous tome on Genet, I suggested, must have made its subject slightly uneasy. Not at all, Genet replied unaffectedly, "If the guy wanted to make a saint of me, that's fine." In any case, he went on to say, about Sartre's strong pro-Israeli position, "He's a bit of a coward for fear that his friends in Paris might accuse him of anti-Semitism if he ever said anything in support of Palestinian rights." Seven years later, when I was invited to a seminar in Paris about the Middle East organized by Simone de Beauvoir and Sartre, I remembered Genet's comment. I was struck by how this great Western intellectual, whose work I had long admired, was held so in thrall to Zionism (and to Pierre Victor, his manipulative young associate of the time) that he was prevented from saying a single word about what the Palestinians had endured at the hands of Israel for so many decades. (This is easily verified in the Spring 1980 issue of *Les Temps modernes*, which appeared with the full transcript of our seminar's desultory discussions.)

And so the conversation went for many hours, punctuated by Genet's long, puzzling, and yet compellingly impressive silences. We spoke about his experiences in Jordan and Lebanon, his life and friends in France (toward most of whom he expressed either deep hatred or total indifference). He smoked constantly, and he also drank, but he never seemed to change much with drink, emotion, or thought. I recall that once during the evening he said something very positive and surprisingly warm about Jacques Derrida—"un copain," remarked Genet—whom I had thought of as a quietist Heideggerian type at the time; *Glas* had not yet been published, and it was only six months later, when Mariam, our little son, and I spent a few weeks in Paris in April 1973, that I learned from Derrida himself that his friendship with Genet had been sealed as the two of them watched soccer matches together, which I thought was a nice touch. There is a brief allusion in *Glas* to our encounter at Reid Hall in Paris, although I've always been slightly miffed that Derrida should refer to me only anonymously, as "un ami" who brought him news of Genet.

But to return to Genet in Beirut: my overwhelming impression was that he seemed totally unlike anything of his that I had read. And I then understood what he had said on a number of occasions (most notably in a letter about *The Screens* to its first director, Roger Blin), that in fact everything he wrote was "contre moi-même," a motif that turns up again in his 1977 interview with Hubert Fichte in *The New Review,* where he says that only when he is alone does he tell the truth. This notion is elaborated somewhat in his interview with *La Revue d'études palestiniennes,* in 1983: "The moment I begin to speak, I am betrayed by the situation. I am betrayed by whoever listens to me, simply because of communication itself. I am betrayed by my choice of words." These comments helped me to interpret his disconcertingly long silences, particularly at a time when, in his visits with the Palestinians, he was quite consciously acting in support of people for whom he cared, and for whom, he says in the Fichte interview, he felt an erotic attraction.

Still, it is the case with Genet's work that, unlike that of any other major writer, you feel that his words, the situations he describes, the characters he depicts—no matter how intensely, no matter how forcefully—are provisional. It is always the propulsive force within himself and his characters that Genet delivers most accurately, not the correctness of what is said, or its content, or how people think or feel. His later, more overtly political works, most notably *The Screens* and *Un Captif amoureux,* are quite as explicit, indeed scandalous, in this regard as his earlier, more personal works. Much more important than commitment to a cause, much more beautiful and true, he says, is betraying it, which I read as another version of his unceasing search for the freedom of the negative identity that reduces all language to empty posturing, all action to the theatrics of a society he abhors. And yet Genet's essentially antithetical mode oughtn't to be denied either. He was in fact in love with the

Arabs he draws in *The Screens* and in *Un Captif amoureux*, a truth that does shine through the denials and negations.

The Thief's Journal (1949) is full of this contradiction. A picaresque account of his early life of "betrayal, theft, and homosexuality," the *Journal* lauds the beauty of a betrayal "that cannot be justified by any heroic excuse. The sneaky, cringing kind, elicited by the least noble of sentiments: envy, hatred . . . greed." Betrayal for Genet is better if it is meaner, not that of Lucifer, but the kind we associate with a police informer or a collaborator. "It is enough," Genet continues, "if the betrayer be aware of his betrayal, that he will it, that he be able to break the bonds of love uniting him with mankind. Indispensable for achieving beauty, love. And cruelty shattering that love." For Genet, to betray is to assert that "exceptional" identity foisted unjustly on him by a society that has found him to be a guilty criminal, but it is also to assert his power to elude any attempts to rehabilitate or reclaim him. Better the destabilizing effects of a permanent will to betray, always keeping him one step out of everyone's reach, than a permanent identity as a crook who can be punished or forgiven by others.

The irony here, and in his later work, is that notwithstanding his repeated betrayals and his claims to dispassionate meanness, Genet's writing also records the emergence of a recognizable and indeed strongly marked social being with real, albeit threatened, bonds connecting him to people and ideas. In part this is because Genet, the character whose adventures are being told, wants his readers to get a pretty firm grip on who and what he is, for all his wandering delinquency and surprising vagabondage. He stands for, and in fact becomes, the outcast unconfined by ordinary social formality or "human" norms. But it is also true that Genet's work is undeniably influenced by the history and the politics of his time; in that setting and throughout that world Genet's addiction to betrayal is a clearly perceptible element. Far from occurring in the abstract, however, it is interpretable as part of his radical politics, which have allied him with Black Panthers, Algerians, and Palestinians. To betray them is not to abandon them exactly, but to retain for himself the right not to belong, not to be accountable, not to be tied down.

Does his love for the Palestinians nevertheless amount to a

kind of overturned or exploded Orientalism? Or is it a sort of reformulated colonialist love of handsomely dark young men? Genet did allow his love for Arabs to be his approach to them, but there is no indication that he aspired to a special position, like some benevolent White Father, when he was with them or wrote about them. On the other hand, he never tried to go native, be someone other than he was. There is no evidence at all that he relied on colonial knowledge or lore to guide him, and he did not resort in what he wrote or said to clichés about Arab customs, or mentality, or a tribal past, which he might have used to interpret what he saw or felt. However he might have made his initial contacts with the Arabs (*Un Captif* suggests that he first fell in love with an Arab while an eighteen-year-old soldier in Damascus half a century ago), he entered the Arab space and lived in it not as an investigator of exoticism but as someone for whom the Arabs had actuality and a presence that he enjoyed, felt comfortable with, even though he was, and remained, different. In the context of a dominant Orientalism that commanded, codified, articulated virtually all Western knowledge and experience of the Arab/Islamic world, there is something quietly but heroically subversive about Genet's extraordinary relationship with the Arabs.

These matters lay a special kind of obligation on Arab readers and critics of Genet, which compels us to read him with unusual attention. Yes, he was a lover of Arabs—something not many of us are accustomed to from Western writers and thinkers, who have found an adversarial relationship with us more congenial—and it is this particular emotion that stamps his last major works. Both were written in a frankly partisan mode—*The Screens* in support of Algerian resistance during the height of the colonial struggle, *Un Captif* in support of Palestinian resistance from the late '60s until his death in 1986—so that one is left in no doubt where Genet stood. His anger and enmity against France had autobiographical roots; on one level, therefore, to attack France in *The Screens* was to transgress against the government that had judged him and imprisoned him in places like La Mettray. But on another level, France represents the authority into which all social movements normally harden once they have achieved success. Genet celebrates the betrayal by Saïd, the protagonist of

The Screens, not only because it guarantees the prerogatives of freedom and beauty for an individual in perpetual revolt, but also because its preemptive violence is a way of forestalling what revolutions in course never admit, that their first great enemies—and victims—after they triumph are likely to be the artists and intellectuals who supported the revolution out of love, not out of the accidents of nationality, or the likelihood of success, or the dictates of theory.

Genet's attachment to Palestine was intermittent. After some years in reserve, it was revived in the fall of 1982, when he returned to Beirut and wrote his memorable piece on the Sabra and Shatila massacres. He makes clear, however (in the concluding pages of *Un Captif*), that what ties him to Palestine is that revolution continued there *after* it was forgotten in Algeria. Precisely what is obdurate, defiant, radically transgressive in Saïd's gestures, and in the life-after-death speeches of the Mother, Leila, and Khadija in *The Screens,* is alive in the Palestinian resistance. Yet in that last great prose work of his, one can see Genet's self-absorption struggling with his self-forgetfulness while his Western, French, Christian identity grapples with an entirely different culture. And it is in this encounter that Genet's exemplary greatness comes forward and, in an almost Proustian way, retrospectively illuminates *The Screens.*

For the greatness of the play, in all its lurid and unremitting, often comic theatricality, is its deliberate and logical dismantling not just of French identity—France as empire, as power, as history—but of the very notion of identity itself. Both the nationalism in whose name France has subjugated Algeria and the nationalism in whose name the Algerians have resisted France since 1830 rely to a very great extent upon a politics of identity. As Genet said to Roger Blin, for the French it was all one big event without beginning or end: the connection between the Dey's *coup d'éventail* in 1830 and the invention by 800,000 *pieds noirs* of Tixier-Vignancour, the extreme right-wing French lawyer who defended General Raoul Salan in the trials of 1962. France, France, France, as in the slogan *Algérie française.* But the opposite and equal reaction of the Algerians is also an affirmation of identity, by which the affiliation between combatants, the suffusing presence of patriotism, even the justified violence of the oppressed to which Genet always gave his unequivocal support, are all mobilized in the single-minded cause of *Algérie pour les Algériens.* The gestures that contain the extreme radicality of Genet's anti-identitarian logic are of course Saïd's betrayal of his comrades, and the various incantations to evil pronounced by the women. It is also to be found in the intended decor, costumes, and verbal as well as gestural impropriety that gives the play its terrible force. "Pas de joliesse," said Genet to Blin, for if there was one thing the force of the play could not tolerate, it was prettification, or palliation, or any sort of inconstancy to its rigor.

We are closer to Genet's solitary truth—as opposed to his sense of compromise whenever language is used—when we take seriously his description of the play as a *poetic deflagration,* an artificially started and hastened chemical fire whose purpose is to light up the landscape as it turns all identities into combustible things, like Mr. Blankensee's rosebushes, which are set aflame by the Algerians in *The Screens* even as he prates on unheedingly. This notion also explains Genet's various, often very tentatively expressed requests that the play not be performed too many times. Genet was too serious a mind to assume that audiences, or actors and directors for that matter, can live through the apocalyptic purifications of the loss of identity on a daily basis. *The Screens* has to be experienced as something altogether rare.

No less uncompromising is *Un Captif amoureux.* There is no narrative in it, no sequential or thematically organized reflection on politics, love, or history. Indeed, one of the book's most remarkable accomplishments is that it somehow pulls one along uncomplainingly in its meandering, often startlingly abrupt shifts of mood and logic. To read Genet is in the end to accept the utterly undomesticated peculiarity of his sensibility, which returns constantly to that area where revolt, passion, death, and regeneration are linked:

> What was to become of you after the storms of fire and steel? What were you to do?
>
> Burn, shriek, turn into a brand, blacken, turn to ashes, let yourself be slowly covered first with dust and then with earth, seeds, moss, leaving behind nothing but your jawbone and teeth, and finally becoming a little funeral mound with flowers growing on it and nothing inside.

In their movement of regenerative rebellion, the Palestinians, like the Algerians and Black Panthers before them, show Genet a new language, not of orderly communication but of astonishing lyricism, of an instinctive and yet highly wrought intensity that delivers "moments of wonder and . . . flashes of comprehension." Many of the most memorable fragments in the mysteriously digressive structure of *Un Captif amoureux* meditate on language, which Genet always wants to transform from a force for identity and statement into a transgressive, disruptive, and perhaps even consciously evil mode of betrayal. "Once we see in the need to 'translate' the obvious need to 'betray,' we shall see the temptation to betray as something desirable, comparable perhaps to erotic exaltation. Anyone who hasn't experienced the ecstasy of betrayal knows nothing about ecstasy at all." There is in this admission—dubious, even repellent, on moral and political grounds, tolerable, if at all, only as an aesthetic or rhetorical credo—the very same dark force that motivates the Mother, Khadija, Leila, and Saïd in *The Screens,* partisans of Algerian liberation who nevertheless exultantly betray their comrades.

The challenge of Genet's writing, therefore, is its fierce antinomianism. Here is a man in love with "the other," an outcast and stranger himself, feeling the deepest sympathy for the Palestinian revolution as the "metaphysical" uprising of outcasts and strangers—"my heart was in it, my body was in it, my spirit was in it"—yet neither his "total belief" nor "the whole of myself" could be in it. The consciousness of being a sham, an unstable personality perpetually at the border ("where human personality expresses itself most fully, whether in harmony or in contradiction with itself"), is the central experience of the book. "My whole life was made up of unimportant trifles cleverly blown up into acts of daring." One is immediately reminded here of T. E. Lawrence, an imperial agent amongst the Arabs (though pretending to be otherwise) half a century earlier, but Lawrence's assertiveness and instinct for detached domination is superseded in Genet (who was no agent) by eroticism and an authentic submission to the political sweep of a passionate commitment.

Identity is what we impose on ourselves through our lives as social, historical, political, and even spiritual beings. The logic of culture and of families doubles the strength of identity, which for someone like Genet, who was a victim of the identity forced on him by his delinquency, his isolation, his transgressive talents and delights, is something to be resolutely opposed. Above all, given Genet's choice of sites like Algeria and Palestine, identity is the process by which the stronger culture, and the more developed society, imposes itself violently upon those who, by the same identity process, are decreed to be a lesser people. Imperialism is the export of identity.

Genet, therefore, is the traveler across identities, the tourist whose purpose is marriage with a foreign cause, so long as that cause is both revolutionary and in constant agitation. Despite their prohibitions, he says in *Un Captif*, frontiers are fascinating because a Jacobin who crosses frontiers must change into a Machiavellian. The revolutionary, in other words, will occasionally accommodate himself to the customs post, haggling, brandishing a passport, applying for visas, humbling himself before the State. Genet tried artfully to avoid this: in Beirut, he spoke to us with rare joviality of how he once entered the United States from Canada surreptitiously and illegally. But crossing to Algeria and Palestine was not an occasion for such adventurism, but rather the expression of a dangerous and subversive politics involving borders to be negotiated, expectations to be fulfilled, dangers to be confronted. And, to speak here as a Palestinian, I believe that Genet's choice of Palestine in the 1970s and 1980s was the most dangerous political choice, the scariest journey of all. Only Palestine has not been co-opted in the West by either the dominant liberal or the dominant establishment political culture. Ask any Palestinian and he or she will tell you how our identity is still the only criminalized and delinquent selfhood—whose code word is terrorism—in a historical period in the West that has liberated or variously dignified most other races and nationalities. So the choice first of Algeria in the 1950s, then of Palestine in the period thereafter, is and ought to be understood as a vital act of Genet's solidarity, his willingly enraptured identification with other identities whose existence involves a strenuously contested struggle.

So identity grates against identity. Genet's is thus the most antithetical of imaginations. Ruling all his endeavors, housing all his nomadic energy, are precision and grace, embodied in one of the greatest formal French styles since Chateaubriand (here I quote Richard Howard). One never feels any sort of sloppiness or diversion in what he does, any more than one would expect Genet to have worn a three-piece suit and worked in an office. Genius ("le génie"), he once said, "c'est la rigeur dans le désespoir." How perfectly that sense is caught in Khadija's great ode to "le mal" in scene 12 of *The Screens,* with its combination of hieratic severity and its surprising self-deflation, all contained in a rhythm of high formality that suggests an unlikely combination of Racine and Zazie.

Genet is like that other great modern dissolver of identity, Adorno, for whom no thought is translatable into any other equivalent, yet whose relentless urge to communicate his precision and desperation—with the fineness and counter-narratival energy that makes *Minima Moralia* his masterpiece—furnishes a perfect metaphysical accompaniment to Genet's funereal pomp and scabrous raucousness. What we miss in Adorno is Genet's scurrilous humor, so evident in his booming send-ups of Sir Harold and his son, the vamps and missionaries, whores and French soldiers of *The Screens.* In both, however, a fantastic decision is enacted to be eccentric, and to be so with unbendable, unmodifiable rigor, to write of triviality or degradation with an almost metaphysically driven grandeur that is compelling, melancholy, heartrending. Such solitude as theirs is resistance and hopelessness together, to be neither emulated nor routinized, no matter how much the reader may appreciate (or appropriate) some of what they say.

Adorno, however, is a minimalist whose distrust and hatred of the totality cause him to work entirely in fragments, aphorisms, essays, and digressions. As opposed to Adorno's micrologics, Genet is a poet of large Dionysiac forms, of ceremonies and carnivalesque display: his work is related to the Ibsen of *Peer Gynt,* to Artaud, Peter Weiss, and Aimé Césaire. His characters do not interest us because of their psychology but because in their own obsessive ways they are the paradoxically casual and yet formalistic bearers of a very finely imagined and understood history. Genet made the step, crossed the legal borders, that very few white men or women even attempted. He traversed the space from the metropolitan center to the colony; his unquestioned solidarity was with the very same oppressed identified and so passionately analyzed by Fanon.

I don't think it is wrong to say that in the twentieth century, with very few exceptions, great art in a colonial situation appears only in support of what Genet in *Un Captif* calls the metaphysical uprising of the natives. Lesser art fudges or trims, but ends up being for the status quo. The cause of Algeria produced *The Screens*, Pontecorvo's *Battle of Algiers*, Fanon's books, and the works of the great Algerian novelist Kateb Yacine, who died in 1989. Compared with these, Camus pales, his novels, essays, and stories the desperate gestures of a frightened, finally ungenerous mind. In Palestine the same is true, since the radical, the transformative, difficult, and visionary work comes from and on behalf of the Palestinians—Habibi, Darwish, Jabra, Kanafani, Kassem, Genet—not from the Israelis who oppose them. Genet's works are, to borrow a phrase from Raymond Williams, resources of hope. In 1961 he could complete an overwhelmingly theatrical work like *The Screens* because, I believe, victory for the FLN was very near at hand: the play catches the moral exhaustion of France and the moral triumph of the FLN. When it came to Palestine, however, Genet found the revolution in an apparently uncertain phase, with the disasters of Jordan and Lebanon recently behind the Palestinians and the dangers of more dispossession, exile, and dispersion all around them. Hence, the ruminative, exploratory, and intimate quality of *Un Captif amoureux*—antitheatrical, radically contradictory, rich in memory and speculation:

> This is *my* Palestinian revolution, told in my own chosen order. As well as mine there is the other, probably many others. Trying to think the revolution is like waking up and trying to see the logic in a dream. There's no point, in the middle of a drought, in imagining how to cross the river when the bridge has been swept away. When, half awake, I think about the revolution, I see it as the tail of a caged tiger, starting to lash out in a vast sweep, then falling back wearily on the prisoner's flank.

One wishes Genet were alive today for many reasons, not least because of the *intifada*, which has been continuing since late 1987. It is not farfetched to say that *The Screens* is Genet's version of an Algerian *intifada,* given flesh and blood in the beauty and exuberance of the Palestinian *intifada.* Life imitates art, but so also does art imitate life and, insofar as it can be imitated, death.

Genet's last works are saturated with images of death, especially *Un Captif,* part of whose melancholy for the reader is the knowledge that Genet was dying as he wrote it and that so many of the Palestinians he saw, knew, and wrote about were also to die. It is curious, however, that both *Un Captif* and *The Screens* end with affirmative recollections of a mother and her son who, although dead or about to die, are reunited by Genet in his own mind: the act of reconciliation and recollection that occurs at the end of *The Screens,* as Saïd and the unnamed Mother are seen together, prefigures Genet's last prose work by twenty-five years. These are firmly unsentimental scenes, partly because Genet seems determined to present death as a weightless and largely unchallenging thing, partly, too, because he wants to retain for his own purposes the priority and affective comfort of the relationship between an almost savagely archetypal mother and a loyal but somewhat aloof, often harsh son.

In *Un Captif,* the primordial relationship—fierce, loving, enduring—of the maternally defined pair (Hamza and his mother) is imagined as persisting beyond death. Yet so meticulous is Genet's refusal to concede that any good can come from permanence or bourgeois, and heterosexual, stability that he dissolves even these positive images of death in the ceaseless social turbulence and revolutionary disruption that are central to his interest. Yet it is the mother in both works who is strangely unyielding, uncompromising, difficult. "Tu ne vas pas flancher," his mother reminds Saïd, you are not to be co-opted, and you are not to become a domesticated symbol or a martyr for the revolution. When Saïd finally disappears at the end of the play, undoubtedly killed, it is once again the Mother who with considerable anxiety and, I think, disgust suggests that Saïd *might* be forced by his comrades to come back in a commemorative revolutionary song.

Genet does not want the death that awaits and will surely claim him and his characters to invade, arrest, or seriously modify any aspect of the rushing turmoil that his work represents as deflagration, which he imagines to be centrally, even mystically important. It is startling to find this irreducibly religious conviction so close to his heart at the end. For whether demon or divinity, the Absolute for Genet is perceptible neither in the form of human identity nor as a personified deity, but precisely in what, after everything is said and done, will not settle down, will not be incorporated or domesticated. That such a force must somehow be represented and cared for by people who are absorbed in it and, at the same time, must risk its own disclosure or personification is Genet's final, most intransigent paradox. Even when we close the book or leave the theater once the performance is over, his work instructs us also to block the song, doubt the narrative and memory, disregard the aesthetic experience that brought us those images for which we now have a genuinely strong affection. That so impersonal and true a philosophical dignity should also be allied with so poignantly human a sensibility is what gives Genet's work the unreconciled and tense note it communicates. In no other late-twentieth-century writer are the dangers of catastrophe and the lyrical delicacy of affective response to them sustained together as grandly and fearlessly.

High River

—for the marriage of Brian and Mary Davis

We were all at the river before it was strange
and toddled to whoops all ribbed middays long
with sisters and kick-sprays, and the light came in tins
but, spilling or strapped up, love was there to soothe change.

Inside water all stayed, shaking; top stuff moved away.
The foggy telescoping cat who dreamed up from deep
was Yabbie, of crack forepaws, fond of waterlogged sandwich.
Turtles, finger-necked, pointed out "One regards one sky each."

Fringed eels, made all of tail, bumped a dog sunk in sleep
and the questioning length fathers shouldered to deep holes
jobbed, and wriggled up again, fixed through a dumb-shouting
kicker, in crisp saliva, who'd be sweet on sundown's coals.

The river swelled through concrete in cyclone-wire summers
and inside the greened rope-tree's palace of jerked m's.
It built bridges, teemed, raged brown miles wide to music;
one side was gorge and hidden—the same side was Thames.

One side was piano balcony, propelled by turning pages;
farther out, raging hulls cannonaded the linen trees.
Moved by fall but also rise to and far round the specific
the river was more illuminant than go by gravities.

The words for field and coppice
are knitted in our brains
and yet the greening river

is a tree-line on beige plains
with biscuit precipices
and clay-creamed chutes like drains
kinked outwards to rocket pipeclay
bums to a waterspout boom
out among squealing childhoods
that flash above a pernod gloom
bottles later will take some down to
away from the concrete room
but it is our language dreaming
and not a bar of race
that what will still a crumbling
walled reach, and shade into place
is more likely than an iridescing serpent
to be a flagged, beamy space
stone-timbered, ringing and rapping,
barges with oars all aloft, stopping
and real water to every brim, lapping
not caked round roots, hiding its face.

In that water-meadow where punt-pole robots on red-tongued horses crash,
stag to martlets, before wowed women, bash, rocking, and counter-bash,
where running with wine and water-skins, servants fluster their final esses
and knights with faces paly wavy chain-boot their baggy fesses,

a table on edge has doorknob cups with wine in circular suspension;
behind it, twin abbeys seat a fair couple, each luminous with the other's attention.
Touching foods with one finger they hear bagpipes and a singer *Ayy Lucifer,*
come away:
Lucifer-Exclusifer, sleeps with the torches lit, Lord of Darkness—by day.

The attended bishop from nuptial Mass is still diagonally departing
when a knight with appletree helmet rides up, his sunbright steels fitting and
starting.
His horse looks where he speaks; he plants a sleeved lance; it too bears fruit
and green leaves,
then, as a share stays in earth while blunt-pointed, but gets worn sharp and
upheaves,

from a furrow of river half-crossing the scene there bursts a mighty fish.
"Gentle lady, gentle sir, we are here to answer any question you may wish,
for I, I know everything—" *And so do I, but I know it differently—*
"That is our limitation; now, the pair of you—" (*Your pardon, I see three.*)

("You're counting their love? That's the pearl in which they move—" *No, thegn:*
an ageless child holds their hands, the one no mortal child can remain.)
"Happy pair, is there anything you would know this day?" They smile, and
at minutely
separate moments, signify no. Warrior and fish exult mutely.

If they had needed lightest addition, or assurance from outside rapport,
perspective would have stripped the table, the Industrial Age started with a roar.
"Odd stuff, omniscience, Fish." *Yes, Plato's keeps guard dogs. Kung-fu, his sets*
an exam.
"How many pinheads will that angel make dance?" *Just two characters in* gravity
dam?

Helipterum Senecio Brachycome Munuria—crazy
the blessing we got from endless lake-floors of daisy
alone, and yellow-top, poverty bush, pink feather-dusty mulla mulla;
the floods spread from their rivers chrome and tan, but re-establish color
in their absorption. The azure water dragon who sustains
most of our nation with cloud and green wrinkles and rains

crawled well to the east, by this time, of our speeding car
as we camped in isolation and drank at the odd isobar.
It was there, before Dodonaea and Sturt's Desert pea
on a sun-splintered wharf a man said Newlyweds? Be happy.
A generation, at last, with no war at all in view;
jets parked with cockpits back, headless. What will we do
with all that human energy, if we've really drained the dragon?
Capital works are out, Identity's near exhausted, Space eats bone . . .
Build a freshwater river round the whole Pacific rim? It's been done
lately, and long ago. There's really only nurture and perversity.
Has the miracle come, the full stop of peace? To hope so is sound—
but bad and unwritten poetry do make the world go round
and God, to save your freedom, must only be privately found.
Had you noticed the world emptying even as it fills up?
Megacities, dying towns. This port ran its own Gold Cup,
now it runs only down. Under the rule of the Horse
people lived everywhere, by ignorance, by loyalty, by force.
Walled towns seemed better cover when the Hounds took over, of course,
but under the Hunt—you know, from first come-on
to pitying looks, that moment of life bounded by scorn?—
Province and Hinterland came back, in a re-run of Greece and Rome:
the sheer forgetting the wild Hunt requires can't afford accurate Home.
Economics? No, trade follows the poem. Work pays for fun—
so why keep them far apart? Turnover is production.
Communications? Indeed! What message did they ever send
but where the action is? And oh, contempt did not end.
What makes us young makes you old! The Hunt motto is distressing.
If your marriage disavows that, *it* is the peace. Take a madman's blessing!
Though the Darling Lily hitches its bulb ever deeper down
in the fox-colored alluvium there, we left that town
for eye-crinking seas of Disphyma, quandong trees and native orange,

and where mansions are vacuumed out underground, beyond coherent
drainage,
came where water drew shapes within shapes, as it relinquished spread.
Myriocephalus Dampiera O Solanum armatum, we said.

Where river re-emerges
confluent from dark
it suckles like babies
it rattles like work.

Mine followed its own shape
its glitter like the flat
of the sword of landscape
and took with ebullience

enhancement from great rivers
of Asia, of Europe,
Callisto and California
which swirl in reverse.

Scrolling with energies
or deep as soul-shiver
in our climate you can
get ahead of a river

an oncoming semillon
disc haloed like a star
with paddock and rainforest
where my people are

their knocked logs a gamelan
to the flute of ever-blue.
Within the water's cliff-face
men rotated and fish too

round a winding central axis
a thread I deeply knew
was woven of its edges.
The great fish could only chew

speech-bubbles now, being
in its legendary element
behind a sheerest curtain
yet though I stood perceiving

the line's long ascent
destroying plains to mountains
and back—each stage looked right—
on through life to my life

my mind rang with a wroth shout:
How dare you be receiving
this vision without your wife?
And I ran, and lost the image

till I saw it flow again
from her pen, as she sat jotting
under snapshots, the names slotting
with both spread and lineage

and in my great dread
of the departing river
I drew strength from her knowledge
that our center is our edge.

Why give rhyme?
It could suggest that marriage itself is old-time.
Since we were hatched out of the crystal Spheres
and real and radio artillery entrenched a Big Bang in our ears
haven't we inhabited a hard knock in velocity
too serious with atrocity
to put the fact that one word looks brother to some other when heard
on a footing with high logics that make all seeming stability
a void demeaned by scrutability?

Love never gave up rhyme;
its utter re-casting surprises never found a kindlier mime.
I am listening now to women who from brew and bouillon of old caste
hoist up on soda-gnawed dowels the huge coiled cloths of the past
crying Who didn't know the cobbles might glimmer out at nothingness?
Of you, the best knew that gravity from underneath isn't levity
but when you were called from broad pleasing and required to impress
you sacrificed rhyme, the lovelier proof that impoverished less,
that added, and skip-turned, and added, on over the abyss.

Cool music of the synthesizer lengthens phrase as it loosens from earth,
it loses stress as breath and dance are jettisoned: it becomes a radiance-girth
a shell of potencies expanding from one blinding source—
who in gravity must be citizen and deal with human difference.
One alone is mighty to create from; so is observation
but rhyme even in language is infinite, at maddening rich random, through dilation
faster ever than dictionaries. Never despise those
who fear an order vaster than reason, more charming than prose:
splendid lines may write themselves blank. But blest
surely are those who unknowingly chime with the noblest
and love and are loved by whom they rhyme with best.

So let your river be current and torrent and klong
as far and intricate as your love is long.

(Cowan-Davis? Good heavens, that's the family we give
thanks to for Christmas. They made the Absolute our relative.)

Myriad floating islands, each a ship of rules
enforced with a frown, a gritting of wrapped tools:

that billionaire's, who rebuilt charm downstream of his city
and imprisoned a Van Gogh for being richer than he,

the dying totalitarian twentieth-century mind
turning in turn to wilderness, telling us what we must find,

the brown drift and fall of derelicts, playing deciduous parts
where the dancing Aztecs sing Uh-huh! Uh-huh! from their hearts.

Bad islands when they sink go down dry. They do not drown
but lie within water-walls you can't see from them, immeasurably down.

From them, it's hard to glimpse the lift or desperate rowing climb
of a few up fluid cliffs, out of their atmosphere, their time.

Your high level sailing draws up many. It is an aptitude
rather like an evergreen fig photocopying its food

or the close releasing arms that let a small child find its depth
back where your godfather on stepping stones rockingly stepp'th.

May the present still be your gift and the future ripe fruit
when I and (it happens) many relatives have become absolute.

SAUL STEINBERG

3 Postcards & 9 Dogs

Bucureşti - Bulevardul Elisabeta

ST 88

BAR-le-DUC. - La Préfecture - E. C.

ST 88

FRANKFURT a. M.
Alte Brücke mit Sachsenhausen

For many years, one of Saul Steinberg's ongoing obsessions has been to collect postcards. The three postcards presented here are from a set recently scrutinized by the artist. What struck Steinberg was the constant presence of dogs, some in the company of their masters, but many as independent pedestrians, minute or peripheral.

During this same period, Steinberg has chosen to incorporate experimental play with xerographic reproduction and drawing enhancement. On the opposing page to each card, a xerographic work singles out the incidental dog as a witness personifying a human event or station—as a haunted presence in a Bucharest street, as a prideful constituent of his provincial square, as an accessory to the disintegration of Frankfurt's bucolic leisure.

Interspersed with this discovered subworld of dogs are six contemporary depictions largely drawn from the artist's New York environs.* This portfolio presents the ensuing menagerie.

—Walter Hopps

Of Dreams and Dreaming

Tell me more about that long street. Actually we're overextended;
time is running out. While still all things to all people we
are no longer swimming in the pool left by the sunrise. No, a
forest has resumed the strict narration. One puts gloves on
to ward off something. What is it? And living by a chair
so close to a thermometer no one can count it is business,
that is, it can't be put aside, and coming out to your guests,
to warn them, is the recreational side we love, that, and all
things, all producers of silence that let this hay
into the tunnel and came out the far side of sleep. Really,
your life is so fascinating. I don't get it. Neither do I—
I mean I was originally the fencing instructor here.
Now my head gets buried in the flour
of reading this translucent page as a vacuum mounts,
and so off to bed. Really it's too bad, though not calculated,
and can never be—Everests of tiny snow crystals would
have to be accounted for first, and that's not likely.

Meanwhile we live in the paperweight of swirling blizzards
and little toy buses painted vermilion like the sky
when it rises up reasonably to our defense in the half-hour
after sunrise or before sunset and likes to, it likes
the idea of museums. Then so much of us is fetched away.
Often you think you can see or even smell some part of it
before it too is put away, used and put away. But then these

so recent nights would be part of the elaborate past, that old
contraption, the one we were never sure about—

It is lively still, playing to packed houses.
What must the present-day analysts think, the ones who husk it
for what that's worth, then come to play games with us
as a consequence of their own dangerous behavior.
It was night over a mountain that seemed to be there, readily
and so useful we threw ourselves on the ground dank with animal
emotions and choked-out expletives: December first! The cocksucker
hasn't been around lately we see through gaps in the dead
or is it dormant vegetation. One of us has to go the whole way now:
shall we draw straws? Don't be ridiculous but don't look
either in the direction of the walrus, the caves of the sea
hold us, though we appear to you here on this simple street
asking so little. The third time it happened I thought I was seeing
it in a new light. Then the follow-up call came. Did I want it
delivered with the sheaves of my imagination, those other ones,
and if so what would I do with these lesions marking the enchanter's
space if he is off somewhere, bold song
if ever I sang one? Though this night I shall untune
the most insistent, entrenched breaths of purpose just so I say you
can come to me, an attack like those told of in time to
an insane purpose that is what we call history; then it will be no nearer
to a resolution, by God, I have to cry out if this mess is what is
left at my doorstep. In the future we'll
have no time for backbiting conversations like this one.
Differences will be put aside. Aye, and rainbows too, slugs
of narrative even the best of which could follow to what ends

in wild weeds, here at the wind. An' if my daughter
bring it over to you there'll be no less use for a mouse
found in your castle and turned out into blind day, the passion
some think comes at night. And we're all over you.

Suddenly it was my time. I don't know whither the watchman
vanished. He told us of the night, then vanished.
The stars are purring in the little Mississippi runoff of the
pure, bulging sky. Ours to consider, no doubt. And what if when we pay
it off, in full, it still runs toward us, too badgered to think
to mention what other tales might have been in store, only the last men
took them away. These were never seen again. My toothache is subsiding
but I won't I guess be the ultimate one, the who-by-definition-saves
what one is after, cornflower that obliges us by never appearing
in the sole instant it is wanted, but is somewhere behind that house,
no, that other one. Besides, when in doubt you can strike a match.

The Beer Drinkers

Think of it as something that is happening
or something that is merely in the way, unnamed
until we call a meeting, go over it, eat it.
And then of course so much more of it is found
than was really necessary. Look at this season.
Trees are shiny, trapped in prisms. Umbrellas
are a new, raw color. The temperature's
not what it's supposed to be yet. Look. Enjoy.
Your house comes clattering down around you
like beads from a string. That's
nice. Each has its strength, its subliminal magic
and knows just how to keep out of the way
until the time for its expression is scratched
into the rude stone. How it will be forever.

You couldn't do that young. Now,
you set about what is going, and already
find it refreshed. And what of the new year?
It had an air of finality to it when last seen
but weathers wash so many of what we are, it
seems lame at last, then crowded into the omnibus
with all the fates, and furies, and us
of course, and the folks from home. How we
managed it yet again is a tale
for the newspapers by now, but how
the wariness of the telling could so

stock a nursery is something that continues
to baffle authorities. And all the colors
put up for sale, were they meant to
go by us two, and what is the change.

They have this tremendous power
in their doing, these Americans, and next you
know a coin extracted from a pouch
will be seen to be the real truth serum,
only you cannot get away just now
and in the autumn the roads freeze over.
And then of course he added distance
and rightness to them, and they came
apart amazed, and he was in someone else's camp
but could write to you. And you were embarrassed
in a bathrobe and it shut them all up.
He was only dying to air these anemones as a truth
and the truth shot all over him
and he came, and of course that one fact annihilated him.
Time for toasts now, darling? I think
rather, and hope I shall see him long
one of these evenings before the new snow starts.

LEWIS THOMAS

The World at a Glance

I contain, somewhere in storage files in one attic room or another of my brain, a very large amount of information about the world and nature, much of it filed under "science," with subfiles for the various categories of research that have consumed most of my time and energy over the fifty-something years spent in laboratories and scientific libraries (also offices, but I doubt I filed the offices anywhere). Trouble is, I can't retrieve the items I need in any systematic way; I'm not even sure beforehand that what I need is there, and more often than not I become engaged in acerbic arguments with myself over whether I really *need* this or that item. The first item, just arrived for pondering on a late gray afternoon, following a session with the family lawyer, is the ponderous phrase "last will and testament." "Will" is simple enough: an honest word meaning just what it says, from Indo-European *wel,* to wish, to live well, with some overly hopeful cognates like "gala" and "gallant," even "wealth," nice to have in mind after signing a last will. But "last" is ambiguous, meaning the latest thing in some contexts, something in high fashion; sometimes a highly improbable occasion, "the last thing I would have imagined"; finally, the very last, "the last breath," "we've seen the last of him." "Testament" is the hardest of the words, needing looking up, something quite odd about that word. Look it up.

The Indo-European root of "testament" is *trei,* meaning three. Sanskrit *tri,* Greek *trias,* Germanic *thrifiz,* Persian *si,* Slavic *trojc*—all *three.* Why then "testament"?

Lurking inside "testament" (the dictionary: "a statement of belief or conviction, credo") is another word with another meaning: a third person, a witness, Latin *testis,* a witness standing by. Good thing, too, for if you are of two minds about the larger meaning of human existence, as I am, it may be useful to recruit a third party.

Accordingly, I shall do just that, enlisting my own witness from somewhere (I think) in the folds of my right hemisphere, to overrule at the outset one of my minds, the one who keeps asserting that the place is arranged at random, purposelessly, planlessly, without any meaning at all. With that one silenced, for the time anyway, I and my witness, my inner inhibitor and editor, can proceed.

I believe, first of all, that the earth is a living organism, of greater size but probably no more complexity than any other attested biological organism, including our own human selves. We, for our part, are the equivalent of cells within the body of that creature, or perhaps something rather less independent, organelles inside proper cells. The whole thing breathes, metabolizes, adjusts its working parts (including us) automatically, autonomically, to changes within its internal environment. Also its external environment, remembering meteorite collisions, sunspots, tilting of the orbital axis, cosmic rays, and the like. In any case, there is much unmistakable evidence that life is coherent, all of a piece: the planet's astonishing skill in maintaining the stability and equilibrium of the constituents of its atmosphere (most spectacularly the fixed levels of oxygen and, *pace* us, carbon dioxide) and the pH and salinity of its oceans; the diversity and developmental novelty of the "five kingdoms" of live components; the vast wiring diagram that maintains the interconnectedness and interdependence of all its numberless parts; and the ultimate product of life—more and more information.

I think I have believed something like this about the earth for many years, but now I take it into full consciousness as a central, plain fact of life, attested as it now is by the hard data recorded by James Lovelock in support of the Gaia hypothesis: the earth is an intact, living thing.

A life of this kind, a sort of immense round organism covering every surface and extending out into the upper reaches of its own atmosphere, could only come into existence and remain there if provided with a constant source of energy and an unfillable sink to assure the steady flow, in and away, of that energy. This is thanks entirely to the sun and the dynamical, nonequilibrium steady state in which energy flows in to our surface and out to the sink of space, a permanent arrangement from our point of view, even though the inevitable decay some billions of years hence will stop everything—but by that time, I like to think, we and the rest of life will long since have lodged our collective selves (self) elsewhere.

This brings me to the answer to the heaviest of all the criticisms of the James Lovelock–Lynn Margulis–Gaia idea. If the earth is coherently alive, it must meet our standing criterion for defining an organism: the ability to reproduce. Does it? The answer is, of course, stick around and watch. We are already at it, still only in the earliest stages: preparing the seeds and their pods for distribution on solar winds, not just in our suburban solar system but out into the galaxy and away. We are doing this with the same awareness of pleasure and excitement that accompanies the act of reproduction at every level in biology, enraptured by the mechanics of space travel without a thought to its end result, the replication of life abroad.

When I wrote, back a bit, that we humans might rank in the scale of living parts as something analogous to cells, then added, in surrogate modesty, that we might be better compared to organelles, I meant as individuals. As a collective species, however, we rank much higher, grander than a living cell, closer to the level of a living tissue. I attribute this status to two of our biological endowments: the complexity and size of our brains, and the genetically determined nature of our social living.

We are, so far as we know, unique among the living components of the earth in having a brain capable not only of awareness and what we call consciousness (I happen to believe that a great many other animals, including my cat and all the social insects, possess the same sort of awareness) but also of something more than this. We record the details of our past experience and make compulsive guesses about our future (much as I am engaged in at the moment). More than this—and here is our uniquely distinguishing feature—we *talk* to each other about these things. In short, we are unique because of language.

But our brain, and the capabilities it gives us, would not alone be enough to set us at our proper station in nature. The really important, far and away *most* important thing about human beings is human society. We are, with an intensity and lifelong commitment beyond any other species on the planet, biologically, mandatorily, ineluctably social animals. We could never survive as single, separate individuals, any more than a single bee can live detached from the hive. We have the capacity to think together as we talk, and under ideal circumstances we can generate thoughts of a magnitude beyond the comprehension of any single one of us. A conspicuous example of this trait is language itself, so strange and new a phenomenon as to pass all understanding. And, because of language, a literature, a body of art, pure mathematics, a feeling for music (the strangest and thus far the best of our achievements, in my view), and, when we do not in folly suppress it, a deep affection for each other.

I said "under *ideal* circumstances," which is an evasive way of saying we haven't done these things to our capacity, not yet.

But look at us, and where we came from, and consider how new we are to the earth, and how young. We have existed as real human beings, by every definition we make for ourselves, for a mere thirty-five thousand years, an almost undetectable flash of time, no time at all in geological timespans. Here, in the last years of our own twentieth century, we could, of course, become extinct at any time, but surely not because of any lack of capacity to compete with other species, not because of Neanderthal befuddlement. If we are to become extinct, it will be our own clever, ingenious handiwork.

We are still young, as a species, still learning our way round the world, and are now at a dangerous age, something like late childhood or early adolescence, prone to folly in the centuries just ahead. Already we show signs of getting beyond ourselves, as we say of children, and in the organization of our affairs as nation-states we have a long record of fecklessness. To our credit we do truly like each other, even love each other, and great stretches of human language tell us this about ourselves. We came from the dust of the earth, Indo-European *dhghem,* and from this antique root we made "humus," but also "human," "humane," and "humble"; the root for being born, becoming, was *gen,* and from this we brought to language "kind," "gentle," "generous," and "genius"; by way of the Latin root *gnasci* we made "nature" and "natural," "benign," even "nation," in our high hopes for the species. But for all our regard for each other close at hand, in families and groups of friends, when we assemble ourselves in crowds and try to think together in excitement, we lose a part of our minds and language, and turn murderous. I do not understand the mechanism of this disorder, and I can only hope that we will outgrow it. We have known about it for a long time; our word "threat" came into English from Latin *trudere* to mean originally "a crowd or crush of people." What we need, for the years ahead, more than anything else, is time, time to grow up, time to learn.

Learning, come to think of it, is really what we are best of all at. Language is a wonder, of course, but learning is what language allows us to do, and learning is what we need most as a species. Science is part of this process. From my viewpoint, professionally prejudiced as it is, science is a very important part at this stage, but not yet the most important. There are a great many things to learn about ourselves, and about the earth, and about our obligations to the earth and to each other, for which we will not have our instructions from science alone, maybe not from science at all. I suspect we will pick up information of the sort needed for our future from changes about our feelings about ourselves in very large numbers, and about the earth as a very large and fundamentally good-natured (although in our terms also very tough) creature.

One thing eludes me, always has and likely always will. If the earth is what I think it is—an immense being, intact and coherent—does it have a mind? If it does, what is it thinking? We like to tell each other these days, in our hubris, that we are the thinking part, the earth's awareness of itself. Without us and our marvelous brains, even the universe would not exist; we form it and all the particles of its structure, and without us on the scene the whole affair would pop off into the old random disorder. I believe only a little of this, to the extent that whatever awareness we manage to achieve comes automatically into the earth's reach.

But I believe another thing, somewhat larger. The earth consists of a multitude, a near-infinity of living species, all engaged in some kind of thought. Moths, for instance, do their own kind of thinking: they have receptors for the ultrasound probes of bats, and swerve to one side or drop to the ground if the bat is at a distance safe enough for that maneuver; but if the bat is close by, a meter or so away, and escape is nearly impossible, the moth does some very hard, quick thinking and switches chaos on in its brain. The result is a series of wild, unpredictable darting movements, and because of these an occasional lucky moth escapes.

Given brains all over the place, all engaged in thought—some of them thinking, to be sure, very small thoughts, but all interacting and interconnected at least in the sense that the separate termites in a twenty-foot-tall termite hill are interconnected—and given the living mass of the earth, including its atmosphere and the swamps and the waters under the earth, there must be something like a mind at work, adrift somewhere around or over or within the mass.

My scientist friends will not be liking this notion, although I shouldn't think they would object to the less grand view that any electronically monitored system of living agents in close connection and communication with each other might, sooner or later, when their mass becomes large and dense enough, begin to emit signals indicating coherence and moments of synchrony. Even so, my friends will object to the term "mind," worrying that I am proposing something mystical, a governor of the earth's affairs, a Presence—something *in charge,* issuing orders to this part or that, running the place.

Not a bit of it, or maybe only a little bit; my fantasy is of a different nature. This mind is merely there, an immense collective thought, spread everywhere, unconcerned with the details. It is, if it exists, the *result* of the earth's life, not the cause. What does it do, this mind of my imagining, if it does not operate the machine? It contemplates, that's what it does, is my answer.

No big deal, I tell my scientist friends. Not to worry. It hasn't noticed you yet in any case. And anyway, if it has noticed any part of itself in particular, this would likely be, as J.B.S. Haldane once remarked, all the various and multitudinous beetles.

The Flood

It had been years since I'd seen the watermonster, the snake who lived in the bottom of the lake, but that didn't mean he'd disappeared in the age of reason, a mystery that never happened. For in the muggy lake was the girl I could have been at sixteen, wrested from the torment of exaggerated fools, one version anyway, though the story at the surface would say car accident, or drowning while drinking, all of it eventually accidental. But there are no accidents. This story is not an accident, nor is the existence of the watersnake in the memory of the people as they carried the burden of the myth from Alabama to Oklahoma. Each reluctant step pounded memory into the broken heart and no one will ever forget it. When I walk the stairway of water into the abyss, I return as the wife of the watermonster, in a blanket of time decorated with swatches of cloth and feathers from our favorite clothes. The stories of the battles of the watersnake are forever ongoing, and those stories soaked into my blood since infancy like deer gravy, so how could I resist the watersnake, who appeared as the most handsome man in the tribe, or any band whose visits I'd been witness to since childhood? This had been going on for centuries: the first time he appeared I carried my baby sister on my back as I went to get water. She laughed at a woodpecker flitting like a small sun above us and before I could deter the symbol we were in it. My body was already on fire with the explosion of womanhood as if I were flint, hot stone, and when he stepped out of the water he was the first myth I had ever seen uncovered. I had surprised him in a human moment. I looked aside but I could not discount what I had seen. My baby sister's cry pinched reality, the woodpecker a warning of a disjuncture in the brimming sky, and then a man who was not a man but a myth. What I had seen there were no words for except in the sacred language of the most holy recounting, so when I ran back to the village, drenched in salt, how could I explain the water jar left empty by the river to my mother who deciphered my burning lips as shame? My imagination had swallowed me like a mica sky, but I had seen the watermonster in the fight of lightningstorms, breaking trees, stirring up killing winds, and had lost my favorite brother to a spear of the sacred flame, so certainly I would know my beloved if he were hidden in the blushing skin of the suddenly vulnerable. I was taken with a fever and nothing cured it until I dreamed my fiery body dipped in the river where it fed into the lake. My father carried me as if I were newborn, as if he were presenting me once more to the world, and when he dipped me I was quenched, pronounced healed. My parents immediately made plans to marry me to an important man who was years older but would provide me with everything I needed to survive in this world, a world I could no longer perceive, as I had been blinded with a ring of water when I was most in need of a drink by a snake who was not a snake, and how did he know my absolute secrets, those created at the brink of acquired language? When I disappeared it was in a storm that destroyed the houses of my relatives; my baby sister was found sucking on her hand in the crook of an oak. And though it may have appeared otherwise, I did not go willingly. That night I had seen my face strung on the shell belt of my ancestors, and I was standing next to a man who could not look me in the eye. The oldest woman in the tribe wanted to remember me as a symbol in the story of the girl who disobeyed, who gave in to her desires before marriage and was destroyed by the monster disguised as the seductive warrior. Others saw the car I was driving as it drove into the lake early one morning, the time the carriers of tradition wake up, before the sun or the approach of woodpeckers, and found the emptied six-pack on the sandy shores of the lake. The power of the victim is a power that will always be reckoned with, one way or the other. When the proverbial sixteen-year-old woman walked down to the edge of the lake to call out her ephemeral destiny, within her were all sixteen-year-old women from time immemorial; it wasn't that she decided to marry the watersnake, but there were no words describing the imprint of images larger than the language she'd received from her mother's mouth, her father's admonishments. Her imagination was larger than the small frame house at the north edge of town, with the broken cars surrounding it like a necklace of futility, larger than the town itself leaning into the lake. Nothing could stop it, just as no one could stop the bearing-down thunderheads as they gathered for war overhead in the war of opposites. Years later when she walked out of the lake and headed for town, no one recognized her, or themselves, in the drench of fire and rain. The children were always getting ready for bed, but never asleep, and the watersnake was a story that no one told anymore. She entered a drought that no one recognized as drought, the convenience store a signal of temporary amnesia. I had gone out to get bread, eggs and the newspaper before breakfast and hurried the cashier for my change as the crazy woman walked in, for I could not see myself as I had abandoned her some twenty years ago in a blue windbreaker at the edge of the man-made lake as everyone dove naked and drunk off the sheer cliff, as if we had nothing to live for, not then or ever. It was beginning to rain in Oklahoma, the rain that would flood the world.

Was It in His Hand?

This story was assembled by Robert Giroux from several fragmentary drafts found among Bishop's papers. Mr. Giroux's account of the discovery and editing of "Was It in His Hand?" follows the story.

We wore two coats apiece and mittens over our gloves, and Louise drove the car with all the side curtains snapped on. The snow swept from the surface of the fields, across the bare state road in front of us in long glittering flakes, struggling as if to rise and, when the sleet hit the side of the car, tinkling like tapped glasses. The wind plucked and jerked at the top of the car, trying to pick it up and float it off the road. We hit seventy-five, eighty. It seemed as if the round world, made brittle and delicate with the severe cold, would break in a second like a dropped Christmas-tree ball. As we came to a village we slowed up, looking for a place clean enough to drink a cup of coffee at.

Then "Look!" I shouted to Louise. We lurched, skidded a little, and stopped in a bright spray of snow in front of a flimsy white-and-red Socony gas station. But I hadn't meant the filling station, and as Louise removed her goggles and unwound her scarf, I pointed out the place I did mean, across the road.

It was an old Colonial farmhouse, very much run down, without a trace of paint, and as the last step in its degradation there were two doors on the front, showing it had been made into a two-family house. The right half looked normal enough, even to the body of a Ford sedan, red with rust, sitting in the middle of the yard, and a pile of ashes against the corner of the porch. But the other half had something wrong about it, even though there were the geraniums in tin cans in the windows and a balancing pile of ashes outside. In spite of these attempts at naturalness, a few mistakes, careless or deliberate, gave the whole thing away. Out of one of the upstairs windows, on a yard of string, hung an empty, fair-sized stained-wood picture frame. Between the windows there was a large toasting fork, and scattered over the surface of the house were a basket, a rusty colander, and a little wooden box. In front there were two narrow-stemmed trees, and on both of them were nailed yellow signs. One said "Delicious Home-Made Candy," and the other "Palmistry, Tea-Leave Reading." But what had originally caught my eye was a long rag tied to a pillar of the porch. Not an ordinary rag, but a width of dirty cheesecloth dyed a particular mixture of poisonous pinks and yellows—the distasteful colors sported by fake gypsies, palmists, and phrenologists: the petticoat of the mysterious, olive-skinned woman in full skirts who appears at every two-night carnival.

"Oh, let's!" Louise said immediately. We fumbled with our numb mittened hands at the scarves and coats. Once we had stopped rushing through it, the world had turned to meager diamond scratches on a pane of ice. Everything looked flat. The only objects that held their dimensions and moved and grew were the plumes of steam blown back from the cars on the highway, and the visible breaths from our nostrils. Two men, looking flat as shadows, came out of the filling station from under a red-and-white sign: "Bill's." Their breath mounted over their heads in round pillars and stayed there a minute after they got into a small blue sedan and drove away. We stamped across the road on cold feet and wooden-like legs.

I thought we had discovered where the carnival woman hibernates and there she'd be in her magenta head kerchief, her painted tent folded up in the hall. But the door opened suddenly to confront us with an enormous, serious Negress in a printed housedress and high boots laced halfway up. Her bust and shoulders were tremendous and appeared to surge forward. She carried herself in a grand, operatic way.

Half ashamed of myself, I asked, "Are you the fortune-teller?"

She raised her head even higher and laughed, showing a plump pink tongue and beautiful white teeth, perfect except for one missing on the upper left jaw. She clapped us both on the shoulders and drew us into the hall, almost onto her bosom, and the door shut behind us. For a moment the combined darkness and warmth of the hall and the fortune-teller completely overcame us, then a door at the left was opened and we were pushed into the parlor.

"Yes, I'm the fortune-teller and I can tell right off what you two are looking for. You two are looking for a man. Now aren't you looking for a man?" She laughed again and tugged at our coats. "Do you come from Pittsfield?"

We muttered that we did; it was the simplest thing to say. "I knew right off you came from Pittsfield. Well, you may be surprised, but I originated there myself. That's over thirty years ago. Still, you"—I felt ashamed again—"I'm sure I've seen you there. Yes, there's something mighty familiar about your face."

I said she couldn't have seen me there over thirty years ago, but it made no impression.

"Scotch-Dutch, you are. And you, I'd say, a perfect French type." Louise, whose nearest French ancestor probably lived about 1066, looked surprised. The fortune-teller spoke well—not a trace of southern accent and in the tones of an educated New Englander. She talked and talked, laughing all the time, about the cold spell, about the warm room, about why she was wearing boots. She kept a lot of hens and had to tend them "like a man." And her glance moved from Louise's face to mine and back. Her deep eyes glittered under her pillowy mass of hair as she tossed her head from side to side and laughed.

The room was small, warmed by a little airtight stove. On the walls were arranged bows and arrows, crossed knives, carved wooden bowls, old straw hats, folded feather fans, and feather cloaks. A square table covered with books and letters took up the middle of the room. There was a sort of path around it, but it was beset with several sea chests, some large rocks, a few rusting bolts and hinges, and assorted furniture. We put our coats on the sofa and stared around us.

A door at the back opened and a white child came into the room, a little boy eight or nine years old. He hesitated, shy but polite. He was very slender, dressed in a blue suit and a striped necktie. His face was a clear snow-white, with bright pink cheeks. He had brook-water eyes and pale brown hair growing prettily all from the crown of his head.

The fortune-teller flew to him and took him in her arms. "Oh now Bob, what are you doing in here? This is Bob, ladies. You ought to stay in the kitchen where it's warmer, honey." She kissed him over and over. "He's been with me ever since he was born, haven't you, honey? I went all the way to Australia with him in my arms, and then we went to Central America together, and New York."

The little boy held her hands and smiled at us. He said, "I can't make the paper go in. The typewriter isn't any good."

"Oh, he got a typewriter for Christmas, that's what he means. I can't let him go out today. The air's so heavy. He has asthma." The contrast, when they kissed each other, was particularly pleasing because of the clarity of his pale skin and the opacity of her blackness.

I said I had asthma too, and Bob coughed self-consciously, a choking bronchial cough. "What do you do for it?" the fortune-teller asked me.

"Nothing much—injections of adrenaline if it gets bad."

"Oh, oh! That's awful—injections. I can't bear to hear you say that, honey. You don't believe in doctors surely, not in this modern age. Why, you'll get to be a regular narcotic if you take inoculations. You know doctors can't do anyone any good. It's all in your *mind.* You just think you're all right and you are."

She cleared the table for her fortune-telling and put on it several stones of different colors, flat and round, and a bunch of feathers. "Say, you haven't been at Bill's place across the road, have you?" We said no.

"Well, he's an Englishman and the meanest man I know. The devil is in that man and he tells people things about me. Last fall he called up the state troopers and sent them after me. He said I had a white child living with me. Well, why shouldn't I? I told those state troopers what I thought of them, didn't I, honey? They knew I was in the right and I haven't been troubled by them since. I've taken care of Bob for eight years. We lived in Central America for two years. I've traveled around the world three times. The first time I went with a woman and her husband who thought he was crazy—but I cured him of that before long. The second time I went all alone—yes, I didn't mind, all the way to Australia—but I brought Bob back in my arms. The third time I went around the world, I took him with me."

She talked on and on, saying that Louise and I "sure made friends with the boy." I was much more curious about him than I was about my fate, and wanted a seance with him more than with the terrifyingly confident fortune-teller. But now she said Bob was to entertain Louise in the kitchen while my fortune was told.

I sat on the edge of a sofa and passed my hands over to her above a hexagonal sheet of white marble, apparently scrawled on with lead pencil. I learned that I liked brown-eyed men, that I ought to write down my dreams, that I was an orchid and I ought to marry a gardenia or a sweet pea. There was going to be a tragedy, but never mind that. She said, "Now you have a good deal of control. You can control anything—eating, sleeping, loving, even drinking, and I can tell you like drinking. Look, I like drinking too, but I haven't lost control. The boy's father was here Christmas and he had a lot of whiskey but I never touched it. There is one thing I can't control—I love brown sugar. That's why I'm so big, because of all the brown sugar."

When my turn came to change places with Louise, I sat down in the kitchen beside the stove and started to talk to the little boy. Louise had helped him put the paper into the toy typewriter, and he was endlessly typing out "bobbobbobbobbob. . . ." There was a Christmas card lying beside the toy and on it was written in black ink, "Love, Uncle Bert."

The kitchen was clean but even untidier than the front room. Two pans of corn muffins rested on the stove and someone had been eating a plate of ham and muffins with marmalade. It was very hot. A large black dog slept on one side of the stove, a fine black angora cat on the other.

"Have you had your dinner?" I asked the little boy.

"No, that's my breakfast. I stayed in bed."

"Do you stay in bed all the time when you have asthma that way?"

"Oh no, I get up. But my knees are weak and sometimes I fall down." He went slowly to the sink. Already his shoulders were rounded and his chest was flat. He turned on the cold water and drank some, then wet his hands and pressed them to his face.

"It's hot," he said. I felt his forehead and he was running a high fever. I looked out the windows to the miles of long white hills and the red crystal sky, then back to this tiny feverish creature.

"You don't believe in doctors either?"

"No!" he said scornfully. "They're no good."

"What is your dog's name?"

"Rex. The cat's name is Inside." He obligingly spelled it out. "Yes, Inside. There's another one down in the cellar. She's named Outside and her kitten's named Middleside."

"What side of anything is the middleside?" I asked.

"I don't know. I named them myself. My name's easy to spell too." He typed "bobbobbob" several more times. "You don't know what my last name is, though, do you? It begins with M and it's longer."

I thought and finally said, "Marmalade."

He laughed and then began to cough. I was afraid he was choking.

Louise and the fortune-teller reappeared. Both our fates had been made plain enough to us, but what about the little boy? We looked at each other and knew we had to leave with no solution to the mysteries, the scribblings on the marble sheet, the artificial darkness revolving around the child. I looked at him, trying to think of something to say.

The silly thought crossed my mind (I had been reading Twain) that he was the lost Dauphin. He had such a regal, self-contained look as he moved his fingers at the typewriter. Perhaps he knew more about himself than she did. Were their roles in reverse, he the high priest and she the neophyte? Perhaps she was his accomplice in fortune-telling and he was the precocious leader.

Suddenly I heard myself saying to her, "You didn't tell me how long I'd live." I held out my hand again and she took it.

"Well now, you can see that all your lines are light. Come here," she said to the boy, "let me read your hand as a comparison." He leaned his head against her thigh as she held his little hand.

"His lines are deep, see here and here, but yours are sort of light. Now that means that you've always got to take a lot of care with yourself. Things may happen. But see his lines, how deep they are. His fate is absolutely certain."

I looked at his hand closely. There were few lines but, as she had said, they were engraved darkly and deeply into the heart of his hand. She was right: his fate was absolutely certain. It was Uncle Tom and Little Eva the other way about. She was his protectress, nurse, and shadow, and he, the hostage, lived in a world of snow and ice.

In the hall the fortune-teller stopped to show us the hat she had worn in Central America, the staff she carried to climb a mountain in New Zealand, a piece of marble she found at the oldest grave in Florida. She spoke of the tropics and the heat, and the things she had learned visiting that Florida graveyard every day.

As we went out into an austere white world, I could still hear behind us the banging of the child on his tiny toy typewriter.

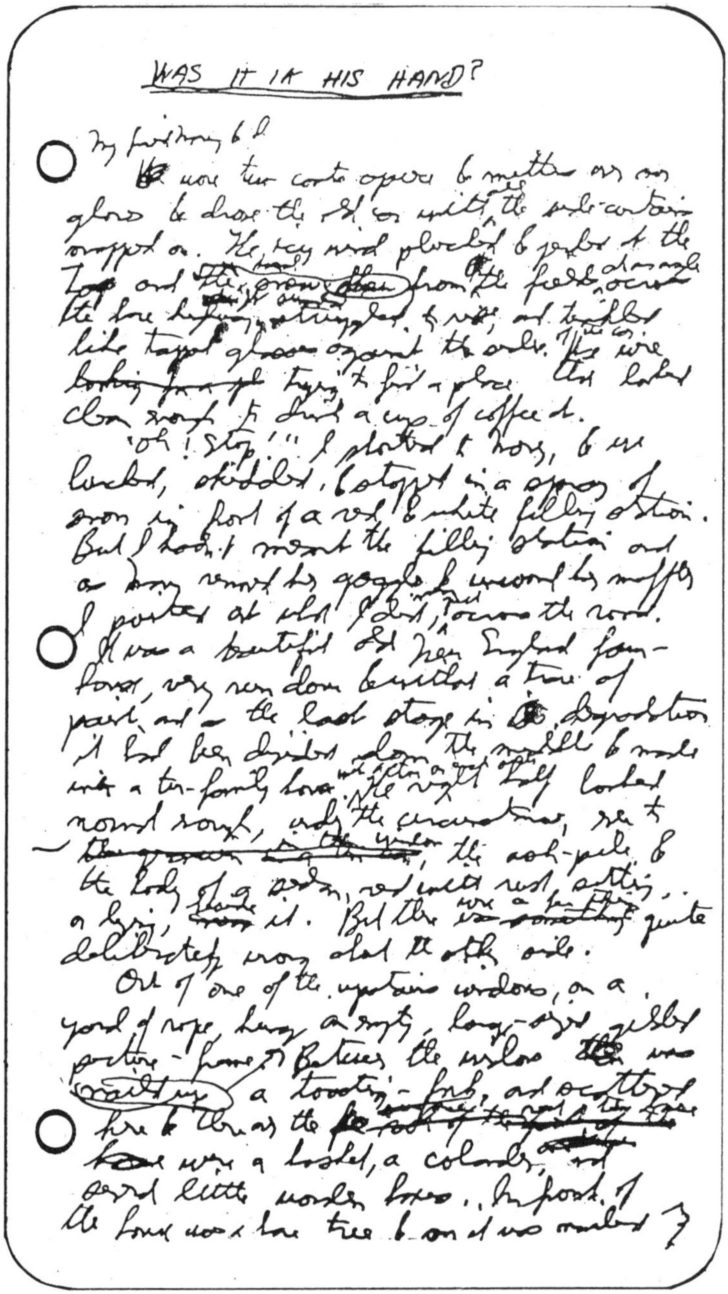
WAS IT IN HIS HAND?

WAS IT IN HIS HAND?

In preparing for publication Elizabeth Bishop's *Collected Prose* (1984), her book of stories and memoirs, I found among her papers an unfinished story with the odd title, "Was It in His Hand?" It was an account of something that had happened to Elizabeth in the 1930s, an accidental encounter with a black woman who had a little white boy living with her. In one margin she had jotted down the words "Little Yves and Aunt Thomasina." References to auto goggles and side curtains that snapped onto the car, and words like "Negress" and "Socony" helped to date it as early work. It was probably written soon after, if not just before, her graduation from Vassar in 1934. Her driving companion is clearly Louise Crane, her classmate and friend. Since there is a mention of Pittsfield, the place is doubtless New England.

I found this fragment of a story so intriguing that, using a magnifying glass, I transcribed from her crabbed and almost impenetrable handwriting everything I could decipher. As with most of her unpublished writings, there were two or three versions of every page, with minuscule verbal variations, but no page was dated. At some point she had typed out the beginning of the story. It was a relief to find a clearer text, though even this version had lots of interlinear changes in her tiny handwriting. Unable to find the conclusion, despite repeated searching (the pages I originally found got as far as the boy's toy typewriter), I regretfully had to omit the story from her *Collected Prose.*

Had she abandoned it? Why had she kept these opening pages among her papers? The story must have been in some way important to her. I finally decided it could well be one of her first attempts at writing a story; despite the unmistakable Bishop touches, it is not as fully developed as her later stories. Early this year, while leafing through my files of Elizabeth's vast correspondence, from which a selection is being prepared for publication, I happened onto some handwritten pages, obviously not letters, that proved to be the missing conclusion to "Was It in His Hand?" With the permission of Alice Methfessel, the author's literary executor, this early story is presented here for the first time.

—Robert Giroux

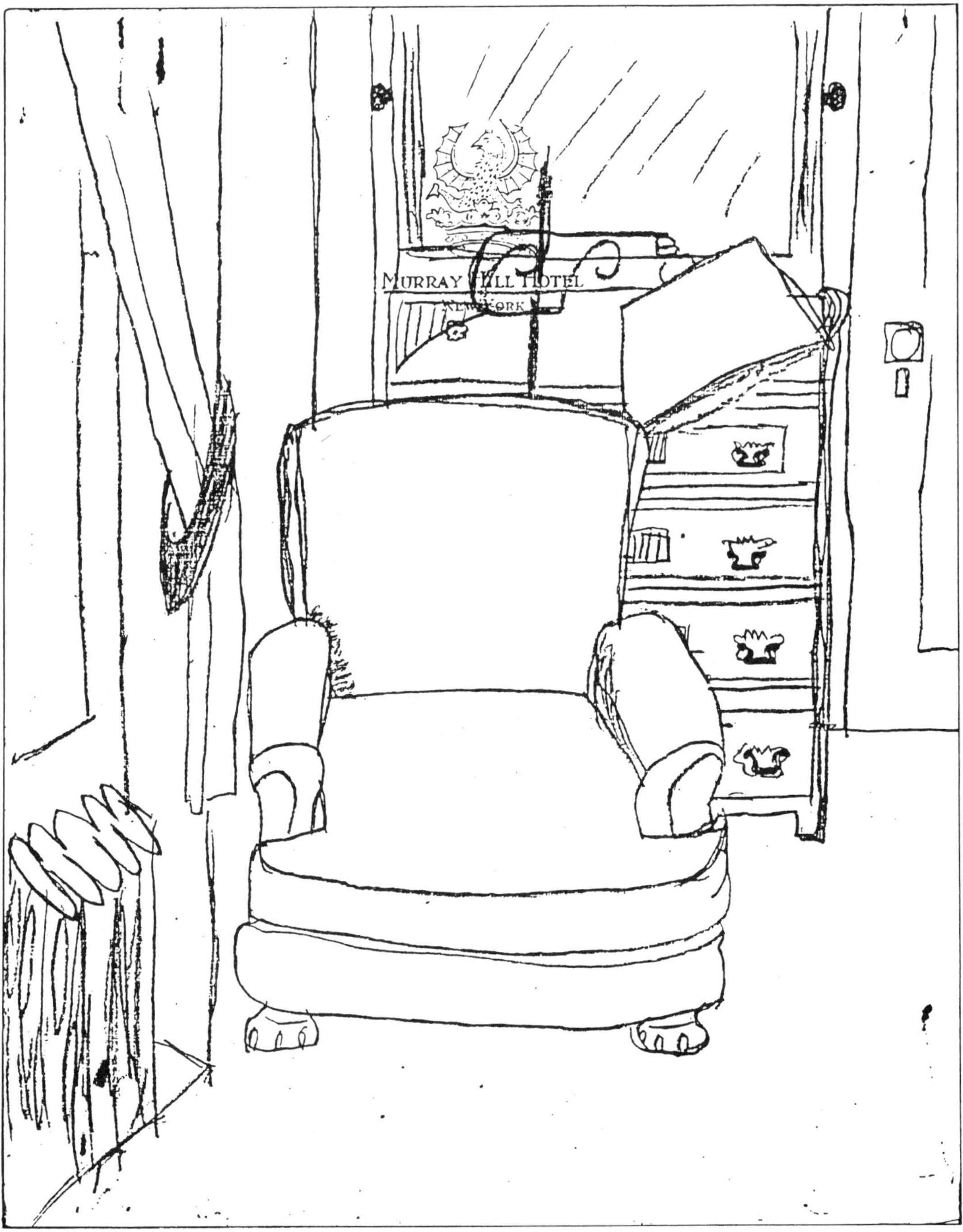
MURRAY HILL HOTEL
NEW YORK

TOM PAULIN

Dwelling Without Roots: Elizabeth Bishop

Denken wir für eine Weile, Heidegger whispers in a cottage in the Black Forest that has been dwelt in for two hundred years by peasants. Such a building embodies "the forces stemming from earth and blood"; rooted in history, land, *Volk*, language, it demonstrates the inauthenticity of transient habitation in modern buildings. This image issues from the imagination of a sinister conservative who identifies "all genuine creators" with those political leaders who are "violent and willing to use power." When the Nazis seized power, Heidegger wrote that the *Volk* had won back the "truth" of its "will to be," its *Daseinwillen.* Hitler had led it away from "rootless and impotent thinking."

How easily Romantic ideas of authenticity, rootedness, traditional crafts, folklore, take on the stink of power politics and genocide. Heidegger admired the peasant shoes in Van Gogh's painting and liked to exchange his academic gown for lederhosen. He enjoyed his walks along woodmen's paths in the Black Forest, which he used as a metaphor for his thinking, arguing that Being declares itself in forest clearings. Walking his solitary thought-processes through the great forest, he exalted *Grund*—the ancient, earthly source of Being—and hated technology. Technology designs buildings, not dwellings.

It is incapable of bringing into being the mystical essence of building, which is "letting dwell."

For Heidegger, poetry is the essence of language. It is "where language *is*, where man is *bespoken*." Language is "the house of Being. Man dwells in this house." Those who think and those who create poems are "the custodians of the dwelling." And the house, the dwelling, has a specific form—it is a Black Forest cottage whose walls are impregnated with racial memories.

Is it possible to contemplate such an image without smelling the burnt flesh that clings to certain German place-names? And—to push the question further—doesn't this exaltation of the poet reflect two centuries of *European* aesthetics? If it does, how can writers come to terms with this tainted cultural inheritance? To rip up all those deep-laid roots like so much worn electrical cable is to place oneself apart and erect a makeshift building nowhere.

Elizabeth Bishop designs such a building in her poems, and a consideration of Heidegger helps us appreciate her rejection of the dangerous cultural lumber that still weighs on the brains of the living. The concept of the peasant from which Heidegger works is a tired one these days; in one of Western Europe's pervasive social myths, a white Anglo-Saxon businessman makes his own peasant costume out of goatskins and acts out the part of noble savage. Old and exhausted three centuries after his conception in the mind of an energetic literary entrepreneur, Robinson Crusoe is leading a displaced existence in England, a country he feels no sentimental adherence to. It's simply

> another island,
> that doesn't seem like one, but who decides?
> My blood was full of them; my brain
> bred islands. But that archipelago
> has petered out. I'm old.
> I'm bored, too, drinking my real tea,
> surrounded by uninteresting lumber.
> The knife there on the shelf—
> it reeked of meaning, like a crucifix.
> It lived. How many years did I
> beg it, implore it, not to break?
> I knew each nick and scratch by heart,

the bluish blade, the broken tip,
the lines of wood-grain on the handle . . .
Now it won't look at me at all.
The living soul has dribbled away.
My eyes rest on it and pass on.

The knife could be a sacred implement like the "aged utensil," a lamp, that acts as the lares and penates of the peasant cottage in Wordsworth's "Michael." In its previous existence on Crusoe's island, it was like one of those implements that are treated as objects of worship in primitive religions or celebrated in primitive paintings. Now the knife is only a dead thing: it is not a crucifix and has no meaning beyond its functional use.

Early in the 1970s, Bishop must have noticed that some fundamental change in the cultural climate was taking place—the colonial optimism that generations of readers had brought to Defoe's text was shriveling as Britain began its protracted and clumsy adjustment to a diminished role as a post-imperial nation. In British pantomime in the 1980s, Man Friday is portrayed as a radical figure by black actors who challenge traditional stereotypes, and to the annoyance of many white conservatives and liberals, Defoe's novel has been withdrawn from school libraries in parts of Britain. For the moment, that text is a piece of colonial propaganda that cannot be disentangled from the stubborn remnants of the worldview it helped shape.

Bishop's Crusoe is a wan and pathetic figure who knows that he belongs in a maritime museum.

The local museum's asked me to
leave everything to them:
the flute, the knife, the shrivelled shoes,
my shedding goatskin trousers
(moths have got in the fur),
the parasol that took me such a time
remembering the way the ribs should go.
It will still work but, folded up,
looks like a plucked and skinny fowl.
How can anyone want such things?

Like Van Gogh's peasant shoes and the contents of that cottage in the Black Forest, his iconic costume will be exhibited in a folk museum where the flute and the knife will acquire obvious meanings: art and barbarism. This is the end of the imperial male, of those "uncontrolled, traditional cries" that oppose "rootless and impotent thinking."

Bishop delights in makeshift, temporary dwellings, furnished with minimal possessions and occupied by fragile voices that lack the ability to make things happen in the public world. The building in "Jerónimo's House" is no stone cottage with an ancient floor sanctified by the dead feet of many peasant generations; instead, it's an ironic fairy palace made of perishable clapboards, a

gray wasps' nest
of chewed-up paper
glued with spit.

It is a leafy, ferny habitation with wicker chairs, tissue-paper rooms, paper decorations, an old French horn whose ancientness is denied by its recent coat of "aluminum paint." Looking at this house at night, you would think it abandoned, but on closer inspection you can see and hear

the writing-paper
lines of light
and the voices of
my radio

singing flamencos
in between
the lottery numbers.
When I move
I take these things,
not much more, from
my shelter from
the hurricane.

It's all so beautifully flimsy and deracinated and benign. The poem has the airiness of flowing script on airmail paper or voices singing on the airwaves.

Bishop is unique among Anglo-American poets in possessing a type of Third World imagination, which bases itself in squatters' camps and shantytowns and which refuses all grandiloquent gesture and phrasing. Instead of the rooted phallus, the female sexual organ dwells in this exploration of "my home, my love-nest." The paper wasps' nest glued with spit— an image varied and developed by the tissue-paper roses and the writing paper—concretely symbolizes the female organ. A man lives inside the house, not like a magisterial poet in a lonely, dominating tower, but as a voice inside a warm and fragile shelter that gives what protection it can against the hurricane of history. Heidegger's peasant cottage is a figure born of the professor's stormy demand for "authentic" leadership and independent power. The deliberately lightweight details that blow like fluff through Bishop's quiet lines are types of that "accidence" that Yeats expelled from his verse.

Heidegger celebrates the apparently natural and traditional in order to naturalize a violent politics—a strategy based on European culture's distinction between nature and society. Bishop refuses to recognize any such distinction, and delights in presenting organic images as artificial consumer objects. Someday a history of the relationship between the poetic image and commercial advertising may explore this type of ironic consumerism. Such a study might begin with that moment in *Don Juan* where Byron presents Haidée and Juan taking a package holiday on an Aegean island:

> And the small ripple spilt upon the beach
> Scarcely o'erpassed the cream of your champagne,
> When o'er the brim the sparkling bumpers reach,
> That spring-dew of the spirit, the heart's rain!
> Few things surpass old wine; and they may preach
> Who please—the more because they preach in vain.
> Let us have wine and women, mirth and laughter,
> Sermons and soda water the day after.

Heidegger refused to be a tourist; he left Germany only twice, late in life. Bishop is aware of the dangers implicit in being rooted in one place, and is simultaneously aware of objections to the tourist poem as a type of literary expropriation. Like Byron, she deploys tourist verse in a deliberately unsettling manner that links consumption with tourism and imperialism. In "Brazil, January 1, 1502," she moves from the image of a lizard with a wicked tail as red as a (non-natural) "red-hot wire" to the entrance of the conquistadores.

> Just so the Christians, hard as nails,
> tiny as nails, and glinting,

in creaking armor, came and found it all,
not unfamiliar:
no lovers' walks, no bowers,
no cherries to be picked, no lute music,
but corresponding, nevertheless,
to an old dream of wealth and luxury
already out of style when they left home—
wealth, plus a brand-new pleasure.

These armed males hum "*L'Homme armé* or some such tune" as they rip into a "hanging fabric" like that in Jerónimo's house. They rip this ferny fabric with their swords in pursuit of Indian women whose birdlike voices are forever retreating behind the ferns and lianas. The symbolism is developed in "The Hanging of the Mouse," where the hanged mouse's feet curl into little balls "like young fern-plants." This is a primitivist image of a harmless, organic innocence that is always vulnerable to harsh treatment by a masculine public world.

With its epigraph from Kenneth Clarke's *Landscape into Art*—"embroidered nature . . . tapestried landscape"—"Brazil, January 1, 1502" points to the consumerist link between colonial violence and art. This is the display of Crusoe's knife and flute, which we as readers admire and extract a brand-new pleasure from. Art and the human eye are not innocent, and this shows in the way Bishop insistently socializes nature. In "Electrical Storm," for example, the "*Crack!*" of thunder is a "tinny sound, like a dropped tumbler," while the hail that follows its splintering smash is like artificial pearls:

Dead-white, wax-white, cold—
diplomats' wives' favors
from an old moon party.

The images delight in their social existence and relish a luxurious corruption. Bishop is developing the Marxist point to Auden's brilliant, flip question:

Am I
To see in the Lake District, then,
Another bourgeois invention like the piano?
("Mountains")

It's a camp moment, an exulting revelation of the artificially natural. And Bishop, like Auden and Wilde, textures her writing with an ironic exquisiteness.

This exquisite aestheticism has led many critics to view Bishop as refusing all accredited political themes, though her poems identify unobtrusively with poor peasants and workers. Imaginatively, she belongs with the "confused migration" of the million squatters in "The Burglar of Babylon." She is against the big houses whose soggy legal documents enforce the rights of squatters' children "in rooms of falling rain." Similarly, her refusal to endorse a feminist position has been interpreted as a rejection of the values associated with feminism, though her poems can be read as subversive of "a most virile presence, / plus all that vulgar beauty of iridescence" ("Roosters"). A lesbian who refused to go public, she imbues her verse with a luxurious eroticism that can be felt in her sometimes exclamatory cadencing and fascination with oily smells and swampy, scratchy, mallowy, and creamy textures.

These lines from "Electrical Storm" suggest a shared sexual guilt and sense of threat:

> We got up to find the wiring fused,
> no lights, a smell of saltpetre,
> and the telephone dead.

And the closing image, with its final bunch of heavy stresses, is moist with a tingling, erotic recollection:

> The cat stayed in the warm sheets.
> The Lent trees had shed all their petals:
> wet, stuck, purple, among the dead-eye pearls.

This poem may be simply about a thunderstorm, not about making love. Knowing of Bishop's private nature, I wish I hadn't read it in this way, but I do suspect that she studied Keats's erotic imagery very carefully and then hid her tracks.

Keats's *jouissance*, his labial delight in warm, gooey textures, can be felt in many of Bishop's South American poems. By contrast, her poems of the moral north where she grew up prefer the calcified, Wyeth-like texture of clapboard farmhouses and churches "bleached, ridged as clamshells." These northern and southern climates are set against each other in "Seascape," which is sunny, Catholic, and sensuous until the eye is drawn to a "skeletal lighthouse in black and white clerical dress." This vigilant Calvinist knows that heaven is not like flying through the air or swimming in warm water,

> but has something to do with blackness and a strong glare
> and when it gets dark he will remember something
> strongly worded to say on the subject.

These lines are an exercise in comic *faux naïf,* and throughout her work, Bishop's populist fascination with primitive painting plays against the high patrician decorum of her verse. At times, these apparent opposites work together. In "Manuelzinho," there is an almost feudal quality to the mutually dependent and familial relationship between employer and employee, which seems like a version of the aristocrat's pact with the peasant to oppose middle-class ideas of progress and equality.

There is a joke against mechanistic progress at the end of "The Bight," where the dredger working beyond the dock brings up a "dripping jawful of marl":

> All the untidy activity continues,
> awful but cheerful.

These lines are aimed at Whitman's populism, and in their fastidious correspondence of rhyme-sounds they incorporate and put down the vulgar optimism that ignores art's formal properties. Bishop's reference to Baudelaire in this poem, like her use of "one" and her preference elsewhere for "aeroplane" over "airplane," may seem to mark her out as a paleface who looks to European culture and is dismissive of the native American grain. English readers tend to regard her as an Anglophile who rejects any kind of redneck relevance, and in recent years critics of her work have attacked its apparent lack of ideological commitment. But Bishop's poems fly beyond the nets spread for them by kitsch aristocrats and spraygunning punks. Her Third World imagination celebrates a fecund mishmash of races and cultures and implicitly rejects a WASP mentality:

> After the Civil War some Southern families
> came here; here they could still own slaves.
> They left occasional blue eyes, English names,
> and *oars*. No other place, no one
> on all the Amazon's four thousand miles
> does anything but paddle.
>
> ("Santarém")

There is no nostalgia for racial purity or hierarchy here, and Bishop's tough-minded rejection of modernism's dark reactionary side is apparent in "Visits to St. Elizabeth's," which confronts that ugly monster Ezra Pound, whose anti-Semitism is frequently glossed over elsewhere.

To call Bishop antiracist would be conscriptive, but we need to notice the quietly amused joy she takes in mocking those blue eyes, English names, and oars scattered along the Amazon. The planters who tried to master nature and enslave black people have been absorbed back into the jungle; for Bishop, this is a benign process, since it abolishes the false split between nature and culture that she ironizes elsewhere in her poems. This is her strategy in "The Bight," where the light is refracted through a hypothetical Baudelaire, whose synesthetic observation transforms the blue water into "marimba music." The marimba is a type of African xylophone that was adopted by Central American and jazz musicians. In this context, it reminds us of Baudelaire's relationship with Jeanne Duval, the black woman to whom he wrote poems, and it is employed as a mischievously miscegenating term that refutes the chill ethnic exclusivity of the scene's blueness and whiteness.

Bishop's imagination prefers to dwell on warm, mulchy images, which she uses to create a type of *Dasein* that serves a generous politics of innocence and merging humanity. To reveal the ontic character of reality is to risk experiencing the oppressiveness of a monumentally concrete otherness, a nature that appears to be untouched by socialization. And that ontic character is expressed in the opening lines of "The Bight":

> At low tide like this how sheer the water is.
> White, crumbling ribs of marl protrude and glare
> and the boats are dry, the pilings dry as matches.

But Bishop smuggles social processes and artifacts into this image of sheer *Grund* by comparing its dryness to matches, a gas flame, that hypothetical marimba music. Her camp wit toys with various *faux naïf* pathetic fallacies in order to deny the authenticity of nature and insist on its artificiality. Like Wilde, she has absolutely no belief in natural purity.

At first savoring, her beautifully observed image of fireflies beginning to rise,

> up, then down, then up again:
> lit on the ascending flight,
> drifting simultaneously to the same height,
> —exactly like the bubbles in champagne
> ("A Cold Spring")

appears to be related to Byron's appetitive delight in marine champagne. But Bishop intends that her readers align this image with certain images from Hopkins's sonnet "Spring," whose risky first line—"Nothing is so beautiful as spring"—she prints as epigraph. Hopkins compares a thrush's song to clothes being rinsed and wrung through a mangle, and he also notes the "glassy" texture of new leaves on a pear tree. Both images identify natural phenomena with human, technological processes, partly because the social stresses of the industrial revolution made Hopkins wish to perceive a fundamental identity between the two.

> I was looking at high waves. The breakers always are parallel to the coast and shape themselves to it except where the curve is sharp however the wind blows. They are rolled out by the shallowing shore just as a piece of putty between the palms whatever its shape runs into a long roll.

This is a subtle version of the argument from design, whose merging of nature and artifice also appeals to Bishop. In "A Cold Spring," greenish white dogwood infiltrates the wood, "each petal burned, apparently, by a cigarette-butt." The voiced hesitation helps to heal the split between culture and the organic world, and the champagne fireflies express a similarly hedonistic sense of relaxation.

This polarity is left hanging at the end of "The Moose," a loose-limbed narrative poem that investigates Bishop's persistent theme of dwelling. The moose is "homely as a house / (or, safe as houses)," and it represents that affinity between nature and human design implicit in the concept of dwelling. Its appearance releases a "sweet" sensation of joy in the passengers, who crane backward when the bus moves on.

> The moose can be seen
> on the moonlit macadam;
> then there's a dim
> smell of moose, an acrid
> smell of gasoline.

The two smells are linked—technology in the wilderness, wilderness in technology—and we would be wrong to think that Bishop deplores the smell of gasoline. Oil is a sacral symbol of dwelling in her poems, and in "Filling Station" she employs it as an emblem of *Dasein,* an emblem that is insistently artificial, unnatural, technological, commercial:

> Oh, but it is dirty!
> —this little filling station,
> oil-soaked, oil-permeated
> to a disturbing, over-all
> black translucency.
> Be careful with that match!
>
> Father wears a dirty,
> oil-soaked monkey suit,
> that cuts him under the arms,
> and several quick and saucy
> and greasy sons assist him
> (it's a family filling station),
> all quite thoroughly dirty.
>
> Do they live in the station?
> It has a cement porch
> behind the pumps, and on it
> a set of crushed and grease-
> impregnated wickerwork;
> on the wicker sofa
> a dirty dog, quite comfy.

For Bishop, the sacred chrism of Being is a tiny container of Esso motor oil, and the insistent oiliness of these lines makes the cement building a "comfy" dwelling imbued with the familial essence of *Gemeinschaft.*

By contrast, the vulnerably alienated man-moth returns to "the pale subways of cement he calls his home," where he exists as an undwelling shadow with one "possession"—a single tear that represents his fragility and spiritual riches. Like the hanged mouse or the coiner in *Great Expectations*, the man-moth is the victim of institutionalized cruelty. A figure from an Expressionist cartoon, he flickers through an urban landscape of buildings that are not dwellings.

So, too, may be the wasps' nest in "Santarém."

> In the blue pharmacy the pharmacist
> had hung an empty wasps' nest from a shelf:
> small, exquisite, clean matte white,
> and hard as stucco. I admired it
> so much he gave it to me.

In this tourist poem, "mongrel" riverboats are mixed in with blue eyes and English names. The pharmacy is blue; the wasps' nest is white, not the gray of the wasps' nest in "Jerónimo's House." A fellow passenger of the speaker calls it an "ugly thing" at the end of the poem. Is it a dwelling or a building? This is a hard question to answer, but the comparison of the nest to the human, technical "stucco" makes it another example of Bishop's gay refusal to take the idea of natural purity seriously. That refusal is a form of radical camp, which unpicks the cultural complacencies that produce images of "embroidered nature" in European painting and poetry. By dissenting from this manner of viewing the natural world, Bishop refuses to align her poem with a dominating acquisitiveness. Very subtly, she questions the power politics that the Western aesthetic tradition so often conceals.

The City in Which I Love You

I will arise now, and go
about the city in the streets,
and in the broad ways I will seek . . .
whom my soul loveth.

Song of Songs 3:2

And when, in the city in which I love you,
even my most excellent song goes unanswered,
and I mount the scabbed streets,
the long shouts of avenues,
and tunnel sunken night in search of you . . .

That I negotiate fog, bituminous
rain ringing like teeth into the beggar's tin,
or two men jackaling a third in some alley
weirdly lit by a couch on fire, that I
drag my extinction in search of you . . .

Past the guarded schoolyards, the boarded-up churches, swastikaed
synagogues, defended houses of worship, past
newspapered windows of tenements, among the violated,
the prosecuted citizenry, throughout this
storied, buttressed, scavenged, policed
city I call home, in which I am a guest . . .

A bruise, blue
in the muscle, you
impinge upon me.
As bone hugs the ache home, so
I'm vexed to love you, your body

the shape of returns, your hair a torso
of light, your heat
I must have, your opening
I'd eat, each moment
of that soft-finned fruit,
inverted fountain in which I don't see me.

My tongue remembers your wounded flavor.
The vein in my neck
adores you. A sword
stands up between my hips;
my hidden fleece sends forth its scent of human oil.

The shadows under my arms,
I promise, are tender, the shadows
under my face. Do not calculate,
but come, smooth other, rough sister.
Yet how will you know me

among the captives, my hair grown long,
my blood motley, my ways trespassed upon?
In the uproar, the confusion
of accents and inflections,
how will you hear me when I open my mouth?

Look for me, one of the drab population
under fissured edifices, fractured
artifices. Make my various
names flock overhead,
I will follow you.
Hew me to your beauty.

Stack in me the unaccountable fire,
bring on me the iron leaf, but tenderly.
Folded one hundred times and
creased, I'll not crack.
Threshed to excellence, I'll achieve you.

But in the city
in which I love you,
no one comes, no one
meets me in the brick clefts;
in the wedged dark,

no finger touches me secretly, no mouth
tastes my flawless salt,
no one wakens the honey in the cells, finds the humming
in the ribs, the rich business in the recesses;
hulls clogged, I continue laden, translated

by exhaustion and time's appetite, my sleep abandoned
in bus stations and storefront stoops,
my insomnia erected under a sky
cross-hatched by wires, branches,
and black flights of rain. Lewd body of wind

jams me in the passageways, doors slam
like guns going off, a gun goes off, a pie plate
spins past, whizzing its thin tremolo,
a plastic bag, fat with wind, barrels by and slaps
a chain-link fence, wraps it like clung skin.

In the excavated places,
I waited for you, and I did not cry out.
In the derelict rooms, my body needed you,
and there was such flight in my breast.
During the daily assaults, I called to you,

and my voice pursued you,
even backward
to that other city
in which I saw a woman
squat in the street

beside a body,
and fan with a handkerchief flies from its face.
That woman
was not me. And
the corpse

lying there, lying there
so still it seemed with great effort, as though
his whole being was concentrating on the hole
in his forehead, so still
I expected he'd sit up any minute and laugh out loud—

that man was not me;
his wound was his, his death not mine.
And the soldier,
who fired the shot, then lit a cigarette—
he was not me.

And the ones I do not see
in cities all over the world,
the ones sitting, standing, lying down,
those in prisons playing checkers with their knocked-out teeth:
they are not me. Some of them are

my age, even my height and weight;
none of them is me.
The woman who is slapped, the man who is kicked,
the ones who don't survive,
whose names I do not know—

they are not me forever,
the ones who no longer live
in the cities in which
you are not,
the cities in which I looked for you.

The only sound now is a far flapping.
Over the National Bank, the flag of some republic or other
gallops like water or fire to tear itself.
Your otherness exhausts me,
everything is punished by your absence.

Where are you
in the cities in which
I love you, the cities
daily risen to work and to money,
to the magnificent miles and the gold coasts?

Morning comes to this city vacant of you.
Pages and windows flare, and you are not there.
Someone sweeps his portion of sidewalk,
wakens the drunk, slumped like laundry,
and you are gone.

You are not in the wind
which someone notes in the margins of a book.
You are gone out of the small fires in abandoned lots
where human figures huddle,
each aspiring its own ghost.

Between brick walls, in a space no wider than my face,
a leafless sapling stands in mud.
In its branches, a nest of raw mouths
gaping and cheeping, scrawny fires that must eat.
My hunger for you is no less then theirs.

At the gates of the city in which I love you,
the sea hauls the sun on its back,
strikes the land, which rebukes it.
What ardor in its sliding heft,
a flameless friction on the rocks.

Like the sea, I am recommended by my orphaning.
Noisy with telegrams not received,
quarrelsome with aliases,
intricate with misguided journeys,
by my expulsions have I come to love you.

Straight from my father's wrath,
and long from my mother's womb,
late in this century and on a Wednesday morning,
bearing the mark of one who's experienced
neither heaven nor hell,

my birthplace vanished, my citizenship earned,
in league with the stones of the earth, I
enter, without retreat or help from history,
the days of no day, my earth
of no earth, I re-enter

the city in which I love you.
And I never believed that the multitude
of dreams and many words was vain.

f
ff
f
ff
f
ff

OLIVIER MESSIAEN

Saint François d'Assise

an excerpt from

an Opera in 3 Acts and 8 Tableaux

Très modéré (♪ = 100) Modéré (♪ = 138) Vif (♪. = 126)
Modéré (♪. = 116)
(Merle noir)
1er Picc.
Fl.
Htb.
C. A.
2 Ptes Clar.
Clar.
Bons
IV. 3e Trgl.
II. Tpl.-bl.
più f
118

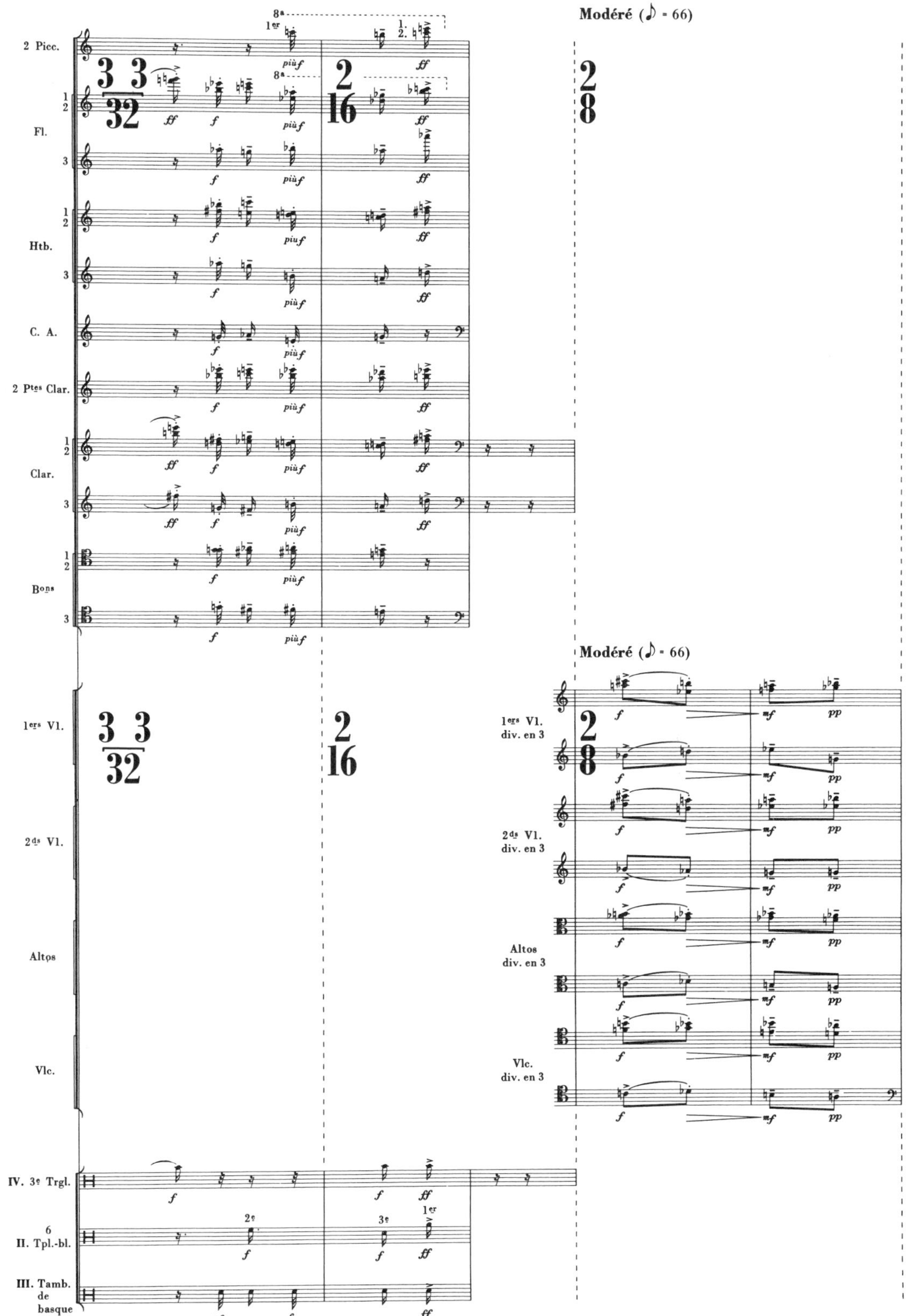
Modéré (♪ = 66)
2 Picc.
Fl.
Htb.
C. A.
2 Ptes Clar.
Clar.
Bons
1ers Vl. div. en 3
2ds Vl. div. en 3
Altos div. en 3
Vlc. div. en 3
IV. 3e Trgl.
6 II. Tpl.-bl.
III. Tamb. de basque
Modéré (♪ = 66)
più f

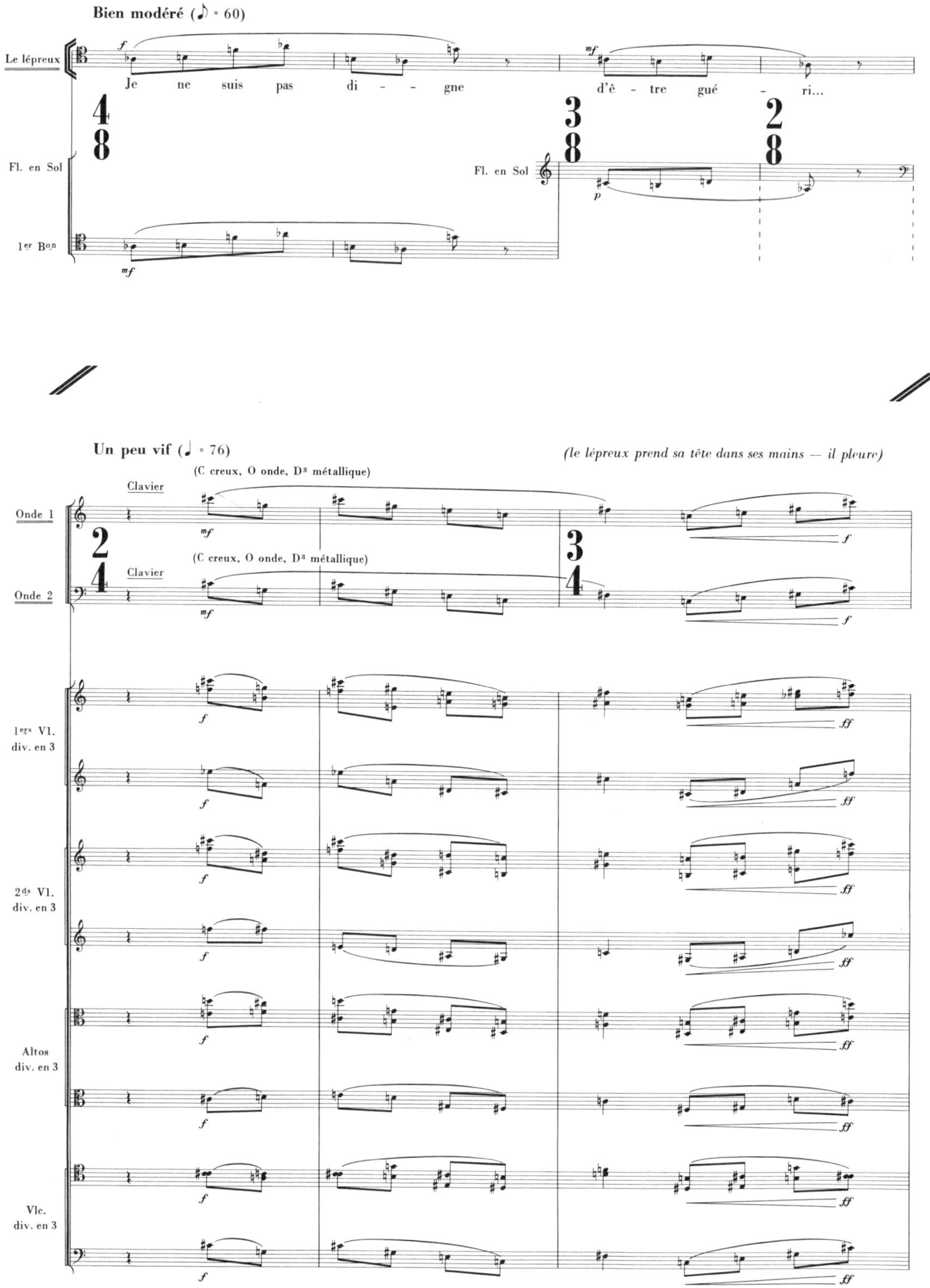
Bien modéré (♪ = 60)
Le lépreux
Je ne suis pas di - - gne d'ê - tre gué - ri...
Fl. en Sol
1er Bon
Un peu vif (♩ = 76)
(le lépreux prend sa tête dans ses mains — il pleure)
Clavier
(C creux, O onde, Da métallique)
Onde 1
Onde 2
1ers Vl. div. en 3
2ds Vl. div. en 3
Altos div. en 3
Vlc. div. en 3

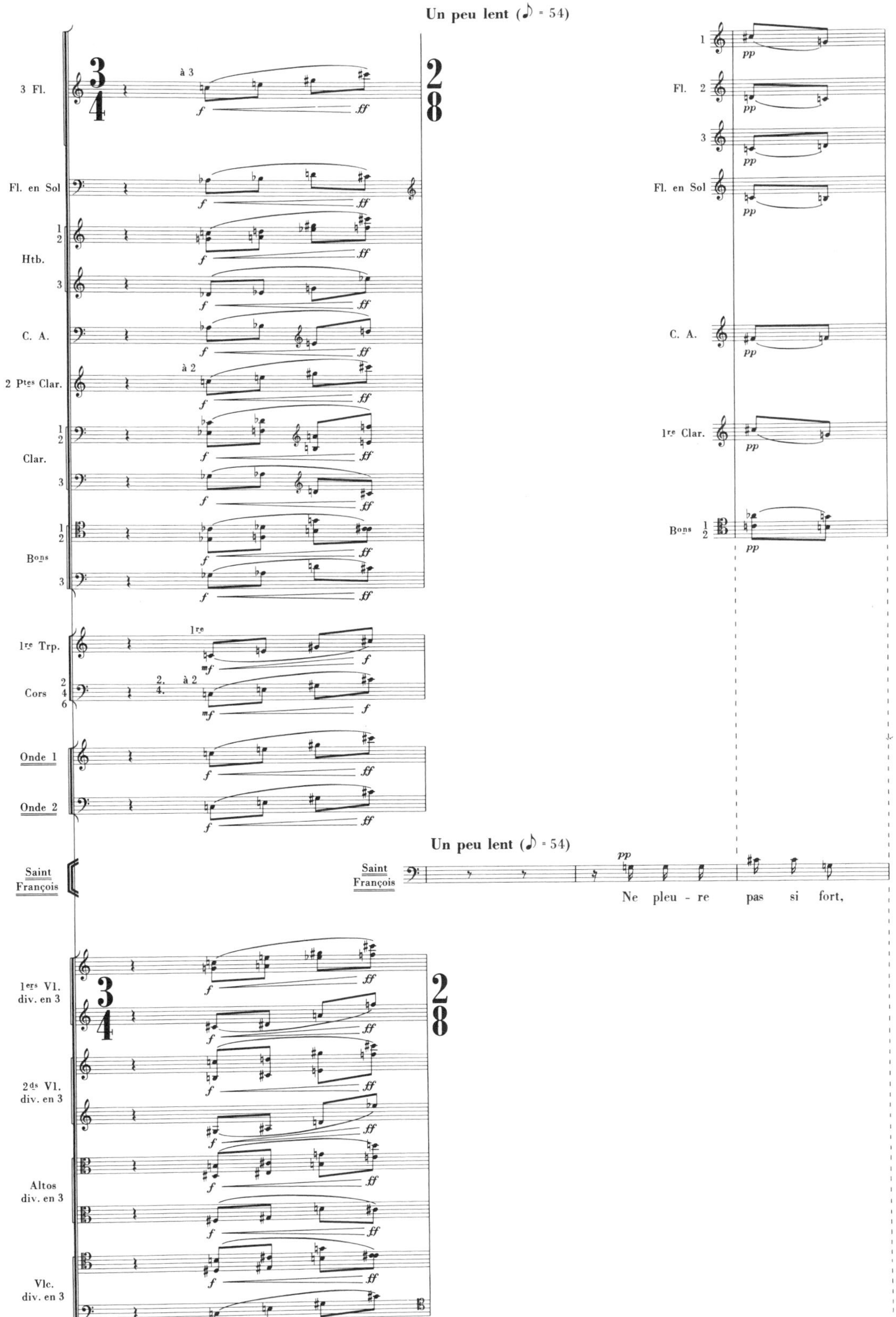
Un peu lent (♪ = 54)
3 Fl.
à 3
Fl. en Sol
Htb.
C. A.
2 Ptes Clar.
à 2
Clar.
Bons
1re Trp.
1re
Cors
2. 4.
à 2
Onde 1
Onde 2
Saint François
1ers Vl. div. en 3
2ds Vl. div. en 3
Altos div. en 3
Vlc. div. en 3
Fl.
Fl. en Sol
C. A.
1re Clar.
Bons
Un peu lent (♪ = 54)
Saint François
Ne pleu - re pas si fort,

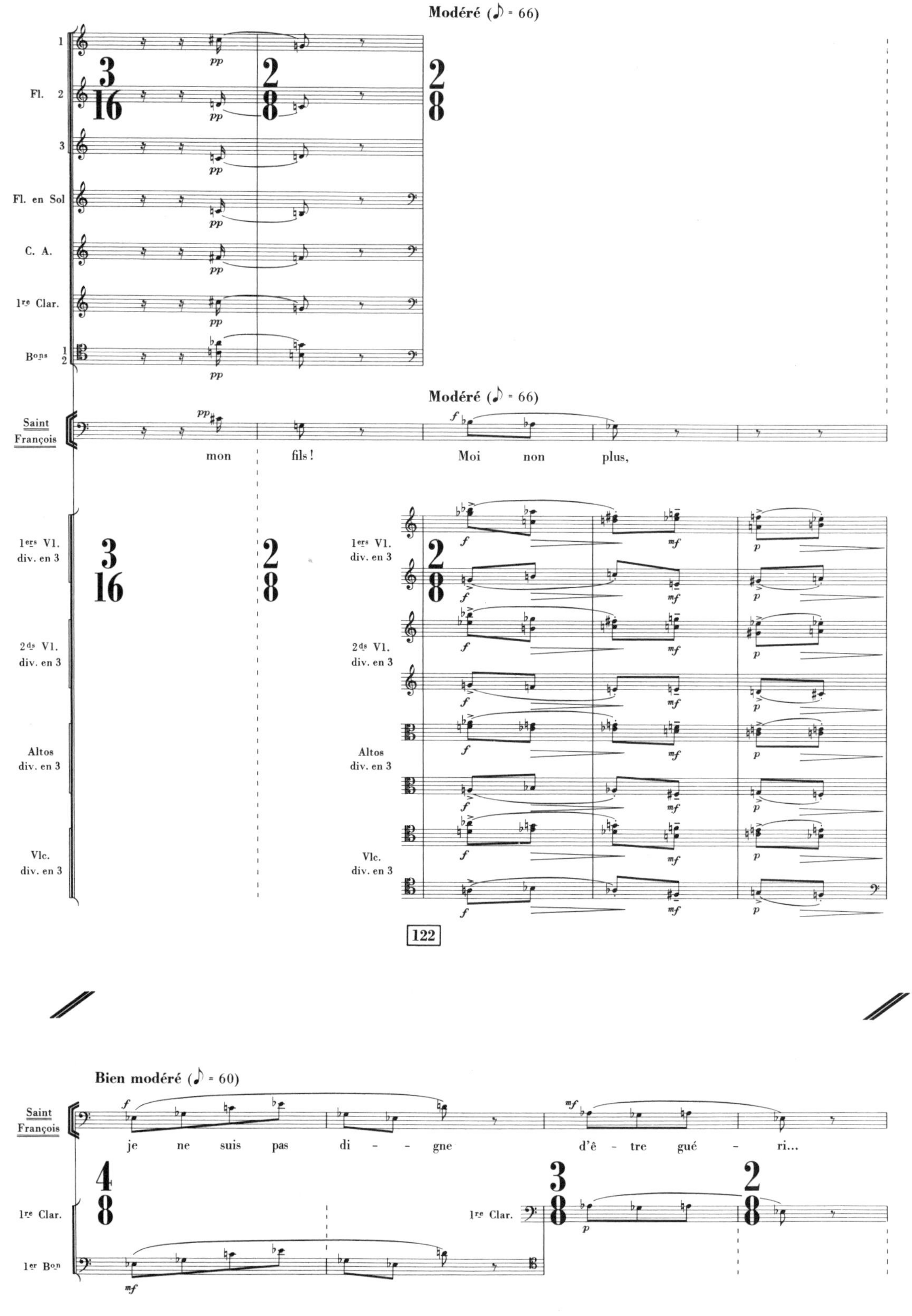
Modéré (♪ = 66)
Fl. 1 2 3
Fl. en Sol
C. A.
1re Clar.
Bons 1 2
Saint François
mon fils! Moi non plus,
1ers Vl. div. en 3
2ds Vl. div. en 3
Altos div. en 3
Vlc. div. en 3
122
Bien modéré (♪ = 60)
je ne suis pas di - - gne d'ê - tre gué - ri...
1re Clar.
1er Bon

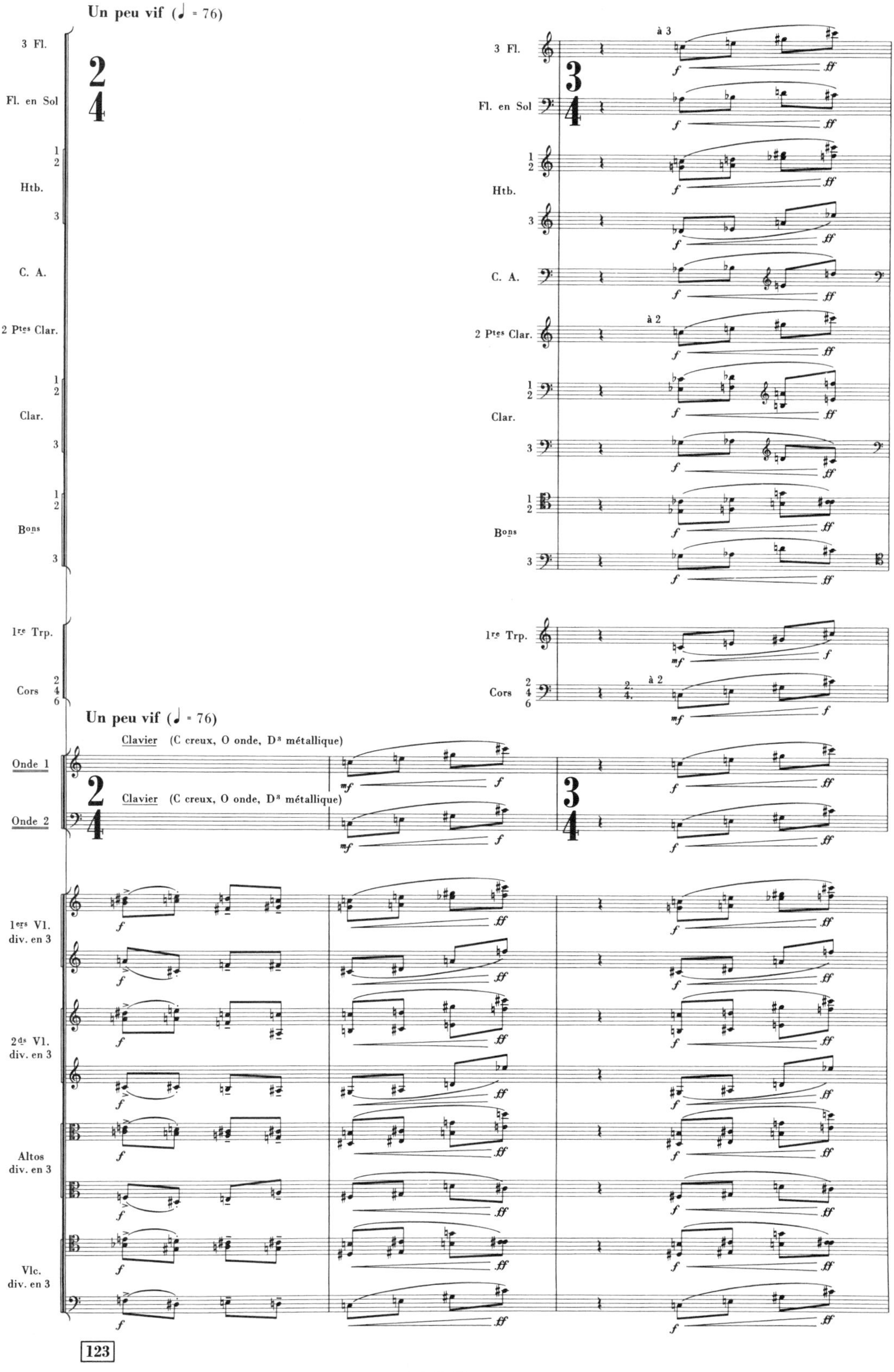
Un peu vif (♩ = 76)
3 Fl.
Fl. en Sol
Htb.
C. A.
2 Ptes Clar.
Clar.
Bons
1re Trp.
Cors
à 3
à 2
Un peu vif (♩ = 76)
Clavier (C creux, O onde, Da métallique)
Onde 1
Onde 2
1ers Vl. div. en 3
2ds Vl. div. en 3
Altos div. en 3
Vlc. div. en 3

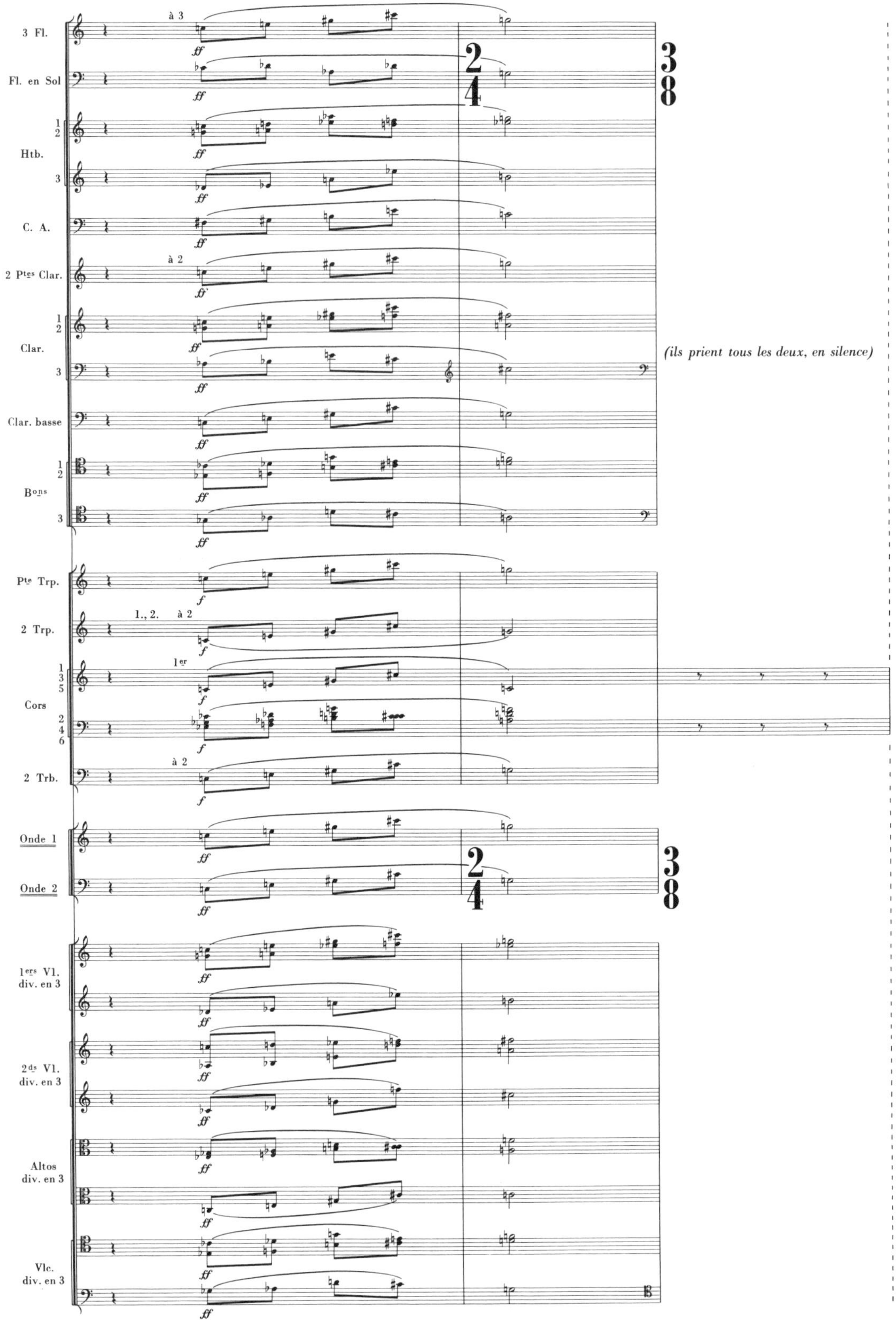
3 Fl.
à 3
Fl. en Sol
Htb.
C. A.
2 Ptes Clar.
à 2
Clar.
Clar. basse
Bons
Pte Trp.
2 Trp.
1., 2. à 2
Cors
1er
2 Trb.
à 2
Onde 1
Onde 2
1ers Vl. div. en 3
2ds Vl. div. en 3
Altos div. en 3
Vlc. div. en 3
ff
f
(ils prient tous les deux, en silence)

A work of devotion and rigorous musical art, *Saint François d'Assise* is Olivier Messiaen's only opera, and one of his richest and most pleasing works. He was sixty-seven when in 1975 Rolf Liebermann, then director of the Paris Opera, commissioned a work from him. Since Messiaen has always been concerned (perhaps even obsessed) with both God and birds, he quite logically chose St. Francis (a figure whom he has long admired) to be the subject of his opera. He wrote the *poème* in the summer of 1975 and completed the music in 1979; by 1983 he had orchestrated the massive two-thousand-page score, which is divided into three acts and eight tableaux. *Saint François* was given its premiere in Paris that same year in a performance led by Seiji Ozawa; it still has not received a full performance in the United States, although the American conductor Kent Nagano has recorded the work and, on the occasion of Messiaen's eightieth birthday, conducted its first British performance in 1988.

Like all of Messiaen's work, *Saint François* is compellingly antitheatrical and takes an immensely leisurely, contemplative, and attentive look at its subject. Pierre Boulez (one of Messiaen's most famous students, along with Karlheinz Stockhausen) notes that the main feature of Messiaen's work is its eclecticism. A fresh ear and mind will immediately recognize in his music a superb sense of instrumental and vocal color—he is the great heir to the originality and brilliance of his French predecessors Berlioz, Debussy, and Fauré—and an unaffected interest in every kind of sonority, rhythmical complexity, and stylistic experiment.

Messiaen never rushes. His music unfolds neither as competitive striving nor as strained productivity but rather as states of presence or enraptured duration. He has almost completely avoided the developmental tension that is the hallmark of the Austro-Germanic classical and symphonic tradition, preferring instead modal music, the fantasy and chromatic digressiveness of Wagner and Chopin, and the ecstatic repetition associated with Indian, Balinese, Japanese, and "Eastern" music in general. His scores are almost always polyrhythmical and heterophonic. One should also not forget that Messiaen's original musical métier was as organist at the Church of the Trinity in Paris, much as other French composers like César Franck, Charles-Marie Widor, and Charles Tournemaire were practicing organists and active composers.

In his excellent book on Messiaen, *Olivier Messiaen and the Music of Time,* the English critic Paul Griffiths suggests that religion and ornithology provide Messiaen with "experiences for the imagination that go beyond the natural: . . . experiences of weightlessness, great clarity and timelessness, of flight and joy." He quotes the composer as saying that "music can encompass an opening towards the beyond, towards the invisible and unsayable, which can be made with the help of *sound-color* and amounts to a sensation of *dazzlement.*" And certainly one intuits such often surrealist ambitions even in the titles of Messiaen's works: the *Quatuor pour la fin du temps;* orchestral pieces like *Couleurs de la cité céleste, Les Offrandes oubliées,* and *Des Canyons aux étoiles; La Transfiguration de Notre-Seigneur Jésus-Christ* for chorus and orchestra; *Les Corps glorieux, Visions de l'amen,* and *Méditations sur le mystère de la Sainte Trinité* for organ; or the wonderful *Catalogue d'oiseaux,* an astonishing two hours and forty-five minutes of fabulously dense piano music composed for and dedicated to his second wife, the pianist Yvonne Loriod.

The pages excerpted here from *Saint François* occur at the end of the third tableau of act 1, in which the saint encounters a hideous leper. Each character is given one or more motifs for which Messiaen specifies both a melodic pattern and a particular set of sonorities, somewhat like an expanded version of the Wagnerian leitmotif. In addition to nine vocal soloists, a large chorus, and the usual strings, winds, brasses, and percussion, Messiaen also calls for three ondes martenot (an electronic keyboard instrument invented by Maurice Martenot that is capable, among other effects, of simulations of the human voice that transcend the ordinary limits of pitch and volume), a battery of marimbas and xylophones, wind machine, sand machine, maracas, glass and shell chimes, tam-tams, gongs, woodblock, and several varieties of cymbal. Messiaen's indications for the work's performance are extremely meticulous—costumes are specified in great detail, as are the angel's halo, the leper's sores, etc. Typical of Messiaen's eclecticism are not only his use of a broad range of historical sources on St. Francis, but also the incorporation of a vast number of birdcalls, most of which (from places like Morocco, Australia, Japan, New Caledonia) have never been heard in Umbria.

The scene with the leper itself, though composed and laid out in vast recurring patterns, is the only scene in the opera based agonistically on a dramatic tension. The self-hating leper confronts the saint, an angel, and his own insufficient faith; St. Francis kisses him and he is cured; subsequently he attains a state of grace, but despite his transformation, he and St. Francis acknowledge that neither is truly worthy of salvation.

Notwithstanding the affecting quality of this scene, the gentleness and modesty of its dramatic resolution, there is hardly anything about it that is operatic in the accepted sense. Indeed, Messiaen has made clear that his interpretation of theater and opera passes directly from Monteverdi and Shakespeare, through Mozart, Wagner, and Debussy, to *Boris Godunov* and *Wozzeck*, and thereby entirely bypasses Italian verismo.

It is typical of Messiaen that this extract opens with the signature of a *merle noir* or blackbird (given to the piccolo) and closes, after considerable agitation, with the two men in silent prayer, pointing towards St. Francis's final lines in the opera:

> Seigneur! Seigneur! Musique et Poésie m'ont conduit vers Toi:
> par image, par symbole, et par défaut de Vérité. . . .
> Seigneur, illumine-moi de ta Présence! Délivre-moi,
> enivre-moi, éblouis-moi pour toujours de ton excès de Vérité!
>
> [Lord! Lord! Music and Poetry have led me toward You:
> through images, through symbols, through the lack of Truth. . . .
> Lord, illuminate me with your Presence! Deliver me,
> intoxicate me, dazzle me forever with your excess of Truth!]

—Edward Said

Antonio Tabucchi
I volatili del Beato Angelico
Sellerio editore Palermo

ANTONIO TABUCCHI

Past Composed: Three Letters

I

Letter from Don Sebastiano de Aviz,* King of Portugal, to Francisco Goya, painter

In this expanse of shadows I inhabit, where the future is already present, I have heard tell that your hands are unrivaled in the depiction of carnage and caprice. Your home is Aragon, a land dear to me for its solitude, for the geometry of its roads, for the quiet green of its courtyards hidden behind bellied gratings.

There are dark chapels with sorrowful portraits, relics, braids of hair in glass cases, phials of real tears and real blood; and small arenas where there is no escape for the beast and the slender men move with the agile steps of dancers. Your land embodies some quintessential virtue of our peninsula in its lines, its faith, its fury. From these I shall choose a few symbolic images as the heraldic

* Don Sebastiano de Aviz (1554–1578) was the last Portuguese king of the house of Aviz. He came to the throne while still a child, was raised in an atmosphere of mysticism, and came to believe he had been chosen by God to accomplish great deeds. Nursing his dream to subject all Barbary to his rule and extend his kingdom as far as the revered Palestine, he put together a huge army, made up mostly of adventurers and beggars, and set off on a crusade that was to spell disaster for Portugal. In August of 1578, exhausted by the heat and a forced march across the desert, the Portuguese army was destroyed by the light cavalry of the Moors near Al-Ksar el Kabir. Sebastiano had left no direct descendants; with his death, Portugal was subjected to foreign domination for the first and last time in its history. Annexed to the crown of Spain by Philip II, it regained its independence in 1640 after a national rebellion.

emblem of a unique nation that you shall inscribe in the borders of the painting I am hereby commissioning from you.

So then: On the right you shall paint the Sacred Heart of Our Lord. It will be dripping and bound in thorns, as in the images sold by peddlers and the blind in the squares in front of our churches. But it must faithfully reproduce man's real anatomy, since to suffer on the cross Our Lord became a man, and his heart burst like a human heart and was pierced like any muscle of flesh. You shall paint it like that, muscular, throbbing, swollen with blood and pain, showing the lacework of the veins, the severed arteries, and the exact lattice of the surrounding membrane open like a curtain and folded back like the peel of a fruit. It would be best to stick the spear that transfixed it into the heart: the blade must be shaped like a hook so as to make a tear from which the blood pours.

On the opposite side of the painting, halfway up, and therefore level with the horizon, you shall paint a small bull. Paint him lying on his haunches, his front legs stretched out before him, like a pet dog; his horns must be diabolical and his countenance evil. In the physiognomy of this monster you shall demonstrate the flair for the wondrous, as in *Los Caprichos,* where you excel. So a sneer shall be crossing the animal's muzzle, but the eyes must be innocent, almost childish. The weather shall be misty; the hour, dusk. The merciful, soft shadow of evening will already be falling, veiling the scene. The ground will be littered with corpses, thousands of corpses, thick as flies. You shall depict them as only you know how, out of place and innocent as the dead are. And beside the corpses, and in their arms, you shall paint the viols and guitars they took with them to their deaths.

In the middle of the painting, high up, amidst clouds and sky, you shall paint a ship. Not a ship drawn from life, but something from a dream, an apparition or a chimera. For it must be all the ships that took my people across foreign seas to distant coasts or down to the bottomless depths of the ocean, and also all the dreams my people dreamt looking out over the water from the cliffs of my country, the monsters they conjured in their imaginations, and the fables, the fish, the dazzling birds, the mourning, and the mirages. And at the same time it shall also be my dreams, the dreams I inherited from my ancestors and my own silent folly. The figurehead of this ship shall have a human form and you must paint its features so that they seem alive and distantly recall my own. A smile may hover over them, but it must be faint, or vaguely mysterious: the incurable, subtle nostalgia of one who knows that all is vanity and that the winds which swell the sails of dream are nothing but air, air, air.

II

Letter from Mademoiselle Lenormand,* fortune-teller, to Dolores Ibarruri, revolutionary

My cards portray ladies in sumptuous brocades, coffers, castles, and graceful, dancing skeletons, not at all macabre; they are well suited to predict triumph and death to delicate princes and hot-tempered emperors. I do not know why they are asking me to read the story of your life, which has not yet begun and which, given the many years that separate it from this present time, I can see only in broad, perhaps deceptive fragments. Perhaps it is because, despite your humble birth, something in your destiny will share in the nature of monarchs and lords: the profound sadness, like a fatal illness, of those who have the power to decide the fate of others, to dispose of men and women, and to move poor human lives across the chessboard of destiny, even if for a noble end.

You will be born in the heart of Spain, in a village whose name is unclear to me, veiled in a black, gritty dust. Your father will plunge into the dark every morning at dawn, reappearing in the dead of night, heavy with filth and fatigue, to sleep like a rock in a bed near your own. Encased in a black dress, your mother will be silent and pious, terrified of what the future may bring. They will call you Dolores, a name suggesting Christian reverence, not realizing that it foreshadows the essence of your life.

Your childhood will be utterly empty, I can see that clearly. You will not even wish for a doll: since you have never seen one,

* Mademoiselle Lenormand was Napoleon's fortune-teller and one of the most celebrated French clairvoyants of her time.

you will be unable to dream of it and will only wish vaguely for some anthropomorphic shape to which to transfer your childhood terrors. Your mother, poor ignorant woman, doesn't know how to stitch together a doll, doesn't appreciate that children need games, for what they need most is food.

You will grow up with the righteous anger of the poor when they refuse to become resigned. You will speak to those the powerful think of as dirt, and you will teach them not to become like your mother. You will kindle hope in them, and they will follow you. For how could the poor live without hope?

You will know the threats of judges, the beatings of the police, the coarseness of prison guards, the contempt of servants. But you will be beautiful, impetuous, fearless, blazing with scorn. They will call you "La Pasionaria," because of the fire that burns in your heart.

Then I see war. You will organize your people: on your side will be the lowly and those who believe that men can be redeemed, and that will be your banner. You will fight even ideals similar to yours because you consider them less perfect. And the true enemy, meanwhile, will defeat you. You will know flight, exile, one hiding place after another. You will live on silence and scraps of bread, and at sunset the long straight roads will point to the horizons of lands as alien to you as those you are fleeing. Haylofts and stables, ditches, unknown comrades, the compassion of people—these will shelter you.

You are dark-haired and dark-eyed, a woman of the south, accustomed to blond, sun-drenched landscapes dotted here and there with the white of Don Quixote's windmills. You will find refuge in the eastern plains, where the deep winter cold cracks both the ground and people's hearts. You have a resonant Latin accent where the syllables sound like the clapping of hands: a language made for guitars, for festivals in orange groves, for challenges in arenas where brave, stupid men grapple with the beast. The tongue of the steppes will seem barbaric, but you must use it instead of your own. They will give you a medal; every year, at the beginning of May, you will sit on a platform beside taciturn men, also wearing medals, to watch soldiers dressed for the occasion file by below, while the wind spreads the red of the flags and the thundering notes of martial anthems played by machines. You will be a veteran with an apartment—a reward for your heroism.

War will visit you again. Some are destined to witness destruction and carnage: you are one of them. In a city that will come to be called Stalingrad, death will snatch away the son you bore, the one real solace of your existence. My God, how quickly the years fly by in my cards and in your regrets! Only yesterday he was a child, and today he is already a dead soldier. You will be the heroic mother of a hero; your breast will bear another medal. Now it is after the war in Moscow. I see stealthy footsteps crossing the snow, a pure white blanket that tries in vain to fool my cards. I sense the funereal gloom that pervades the city. At the carriage-stops, everyone stares at the ground to avoid meeting their neighbor's eyes.

And you too will be cautious, coming home in the evening, for this is a suspicious time. At night you will wake with a start, soaked in sweat, mistrusting your own loyalty, since the worst heresy is to believe oneself in possession of the truth, and pride has brought down many. You will search your conscience long and critically. And meanwhile, where have your old comrades ended up? Vanished, all of them. You will toss and turn in the bed; the sheets will be briars. Outside it is bitterly cold; how can the pillow burn so fiercely?

"All traitors?"

"All of them."

"Even Francisco, who laughed like a child and sang the *romancero?*"

"Even Francisco."

"Even El Campesino, who wept with you over your dead?"

Yes, even El Campesino—he's cleaning Moscow's toilets now. And your short sleep will already be over. You are sitting on your bed, staring into the shadows (you always leave a night-light on—you can't bear the darkness), eyes fixed on the opposite wall. But what else can you do? South America is too far away, and besides, they won't let La Pasionaria leave the friendly borders of Russia.

So you decide it's best to cling to your ideals, make of them an even stronger faith, stronger, and stronger, and stronger still. And after all, time is passing. Slowly, very slowly, but all things do pass. Men pass away, and suffering, and disasters. You too already will have almost passed away, and that will be a source of subtle, secret comfort. The meager bun of your hair will turn white with age and grief. Your face will be dry, ascetic, with two hollows. Then your king will die too. You will stay beside the coffin in the middle of the square, day and night, always wholly yourself, silent, unbending, your eyes always open, while a huge crowd files mutely by the embalmed corpse. Priestly, statuesque, carved in stone—"That is La Pasionaria," people will think when they see you, and here and there a father will point you out to his son. And all the while, to keep from giving way to the panic and heartache that have undermined your spirit, the hands in your lap keep twisting and tying your handkerchief into a knot. (How odd: why are your hands stroking that round wad?) And in your mind you see a room that time has carried away: a crude iron bed and a tiny Dolores, frightened and ill, with feverish eyes, calling plaintively, "Mamaita, el jugete . . . Mamaita, por favor, el jugete . . ." And your mother gets up from her chair and makes you a simple doll by knotting the corners of her brown handkerchief.

Many more years await you, but they will be all the same. Dolores Ibarruri, when you look into your mirror you will see the image of La Pasionaria, which never changes.

Then one day, perhaps, you will read my letter. Or you won't read it, but this will not have the slightest importance, because you will be old and everything will already have been. Because if life could go back and be different from what has been, it would annihilate time and the succession of causes and effects that are life itself, and that would be absurd. And my cards, Dolores, cannot change what, since it has to be, has already been.

III

Letter from Calypso, a nymph, to Odysseus, King of Ithaca

Purple and swollen like secret flesh are the petals of Ogygia's flowers; brief showers, soft and warm, feed the bright green of her woods; no winter troubles the waters of her streams.

Barely the blink of an eye has passed since your departure, which seems so remote to you, and your voice calling farewell to me from the sea still wounds my divine hearing in this impassable now. Every day I watch the sun's chariot race across the sky and I follow its course toward your west; I look at my unchanging white hands; I trace a mark in the sand with a twig, like a sign of some futile reckoning, and then I erase it. And I have made and erased thousands of marks: the gesture is the same, the sand is the same, I am the same. And everything else.

But you, instead, live in change. Your hands have become bony, with protruding knuckles; the firm blue veins that ran across them have come to resemble the knotty rigging of your ship, and if a child plays with them, the blue ropes slither away under the skin and the child laughs and measures the smallness of his own small hand against your palm. Then you lift him from your knees and set him on the ground, because a memory of long ago has captured you and a shadow has crossed your face. But he runs around you shouting happily, and at once you pick him up again and sit him on the table in front of you. Something deep, something that can't be put into words is happening, and you intuitively grasp time's substance in the passing down of the flesh.

But what is the substance of time, and where does it form, if everything is fixed, unchanging, one? At night I gaze at the spaces between the stars, I see the boundless void, and what overwhelms you humans and sweeps you away is here only one fixed moment, without beginning or end.

Oh, Odysseus, to be able to escape this eternal green! To be able to follow the leaves as they yellow and fall, to live the moment with them! To know that I am mortal!

I envy your old age and I long for it; that is the form my love for you takes. And I dream of another Calypso, old and gray and feeble, and I dream of feeling my strength dwindling, of feeling every day a little closer to the Great Circle where everything returns and revolves, of dispersing the atoms that make up this woman's body I call Calypso. And instead I remain here, staring at the sea as it ebbs and flows, feeling like its reflection, suffering this weariness of being that devours me and will never be appeased, and the empty terror of eternity.

Translated by Tim Parks

Anastasia, Purdy Group Home

A man has entered the room.
He is a ladykiller. A real one:
growing smaller and larger and more wonderful and terrible.
His stomach opens, the room fills
with ladykillers.
They are eating you up with their eyes.

The nurse gives you twenty milligrams of Haldol.
Most of the ladykillers leave but there is one left.
You point to him and say, "I get carried away,"
meaning that he has come to steal you.

Anastasia, on this night
you pass out half a carton of cigarettes
and tell me that you will not live
to see another day.

At nine in the morning I try to wake you.
I say your name, I rock you back and forth.
You open one eye
and say, "What you touching my hip bone for,
you going to make soup?"

You are pleased to meet me.
May you ask who I am?
Am I your parent or savior?
A husband? Do I think
you will be a melt-as-you-go wife?

Anastasia, you are beautiful:
rotten teeth, rosary beads, the dresses you wear when you sleep.
I will give you your Haldol, your Xanax
an hour late.
We will walk to the store for more cigarettes.

Flight

In the field, birds rising black against the sun.
You say they are ravens. They should be careful.
If one of them opens its wings too wide
all of the light in the world will be blotted out forever.

WELL, ALMOST.
BUT HE COULD NOT CREATE CRACK EX NIHILO.
THERE HAD TO BE
SOMEBODY WHOM HE BOUGHT IT FROM,
SOMEBODY WHO COULD CRUSH HIM
IF HE CROSSED UP OR DIDN'T PAY,
SOMEBODY WHO HAD MADE HIM.

I JUST GIVE 'EM A SNIFF OF CRACK, GIVE IT
AWAY TO 'EM YOU KNOW. AND THEN THEY GO
OH I DIDN'T GET THAT SNIFF
AND THEN I GET HARD. WITH
THE BITCHES SAY OH YES YOU
DID BUT I'M LATE FOR AN
IMPORTANT 'POINTMENT
GOTTA BE GOIN' SO LONG BITCH,
AND THEN THE BITCH GOES NO NO
WAIT AND THEN
I GO ALL RIGHT YOU CAN HAVE
ANOTHER BUT NOT
BEFORE YOU
SUCK ME

AND I'M TELLING YOU
I NEVER USED A RUBBER IN MY LIFE
WAS HE GOD?

JENNY DUCKED AWAY FROM HIM WITH WIDE EYES
AND HER MOUTH FELL OPEN AND SHE FORGOT TO
DAB AT HER EYES AND
THE GERMAN JUST STOOD THERE WITH HIS HANDS ON
HIS HIPS, GLORYING IN TAWS, AND THE GERMAN
SAID QUIETLY
AS HE POINTED TO THE SHATTERED TRUNK,
NOW TAWS

Divine Men

By their tombs we know them . . .

"The Eternal Etruscans,"
National Geographic (June 1988)

Everyone that I know would like to be God. Everyone is *almost* God. If there is a God, shall we praise Him or blame Him that this is so? (If I had the answer to this I would be God and I would not have to tell stories.) —"You desire to be filled with the supreme Good," says one writer, putting these words into the mouth of Christ, "but you cannot attain this blessing now. I am that Good; wait for me. . . ."* —I have been waiting all my life, and (by definition, I suppose) will have to wait at least until the end. In the meantime, there are stories to be told, for I have seen Him on this earth.

* Thomas à Kempis, *The Imitation of Christ* (ca. 1413). I quote the translation by Leo Sherley-Price (New York: Penguin, 1952), p. 160.

1

DECLASSIFIED ARMY FOOTAGE

(25 MAY 1970 AIRSTRIKES REPORT)

A man in a plane flew along the horizon, firing bullets. The casings glittered in the sun as they spattered against his shoulders and fell down into the sky. —A plane was rushing low, with many little white globes of fire speeding ahead even faster to show it the way. —A plane hovered over a river for a long time, until you came to believe that the plane was like a cloud. Then, shockingly, a white bar of light fell out of the plane and exploded. A soldier shot bullets and bullets at the village across the river. White dots sped away from the plane across the sky; they fell and became death. —There was a plane and a long white whirl of bombs, the jungle turning red and pink, and white puffs bursting at random, white mushroom puffs, new ones forming between old craters, their fire-rings expanding and thinning with tremendous speed. White gobs of napalm fell. Bombs turned end over end, forever it seemed, falling forward as well as down, until at last they burst, sometimes just missing houses and roads, sometimes not; and the frame of reference kept sweeping on as the plane flew on so that whatever happened happened far behind in an unreal patchwork of green and brown, the junglescape unrolling steadily like a magic carpet into which the plane wove its bullet-trails so that it would be able to rise above itself.

Was the soldier God? —No, because he would never know exactly what he had done.

2

A man with a hooded face walked in an alley crying *Coke! Coke! Coke! Smoke! Smoke! Smoke! Smoke!* and I said oh no thanks man that's not my thing and the pusher said aw c'mon got some heavy-duty rock for you to try and I said no that's OK. The pusher said watcha tryin' to do then get your dick wet? and I said that's right and the pusher said listen I don't ever pay for no pussy; I just give 'em a sniff of crack, give it away to 'em, you know, and then they go *oh* I didn't *get* that sniff and then I get *hard* with the bitches and say oh yes you did but I'm late for an important 'pointment gotta be goin' so long bitch, and then the bitch goes no no wait, and then I go all right you can have another but not before you suck me, and man I'm telling you I never used a rubber in my life.

Was *he* God? —Well, almost. But he could not create crack *ex nihilo.* There had to be Somebody Whom he bought it from, Somebody Who could crush him if he crossed up or didn't pay, Somebody Who had made him.

3

Once when my sweetheart Jenny backed up into a package truck and destroyed her car's backside and sat sobbing hysterically, I said well Jenny let's look in the yellow pages and see who can fix it. There was a body shop not too far away, and we drove mournfully down the street, with glass-shards tinkling so musically out of the rear window to gleam like mica on the asphalt. We turned the corner and ascended the ramp from the tire shop to the body shop where it was cool and greasy and professional and very very serious. The German came over and inspected the car, sighing and shaking his head to let us know in advance that Jenny's little mistake would cost her, and Jenny got out and I got out and the German walked around the car very slowly, and we followed him with reverence, and he said eighteen hundred and Jenny shrieked no way! and the German said well if we use salvaged parts I can make it thirteen hundred and once we repaint it no one will be able to tell the difference and Jenny sobbed can't *believe* it! I was just gonna sell it! and the German led us around the car again and said yes Miss you are lucky twelve hundred yes and Jenny said twelve hundred! And I took it to a 'spectable joint! So pissed off! Well, I'll just pass on costs to whomever I sell. —So it was settled. —Jenny and I started to take everything out of the car, maps and scattered cassettes and both boxes of kleenex (one of which Jenny was now drawing from to dab her eyes, kleenex after kleenex with marvelous regularity), as the German accepted the keys into his hands with stern authority. There remained some books in the trunk, but that had been half-crushed by its rendezvous with the package truck and pinched more forbiddingly shut than the entrance to some brass tomb of the sixteenth century, so Jenny started crying again and said what are we gonna *do* about this? but the German said do not worry Miss and the German said Jaws! Come here, Jaws! and Jaws looked over from behind another naked automobile and came striding up to us, wiping his hands on the knees of his coveralls, and he was very tall and wore dark sunglasses even here where the lighting was not so bright and his face was pimply and he grinned and his teeth were full of fillings and he wore shiny black boots like a thug although there was grease on them now as there was all over his coveralls and he came close to us nodding and looking at us with no thought of intimidating us but Jenny ducked away from him with wide eyes and her mouth fell open and she forgot to dab at her eyes and the German just stood there with his hands on his hips, glorying in Jaws, and the German said quietly now Jaws as he pointed to the shattered trunk, and Jaws walked up to it and ran his tongue across his lips smiling and took the trunk lid in one hand and the bumper in the other and flexed his arms a little and there was a sound of metal going *urrrrrrrrrrrrrrrrrrrrrrreeeeeeech!* and then something went *spoingg!* and the trunk flew open and Jaws was not sweating, not a bit.

Was Jaws God? —After all, the German owned him; the German could fire him at any time. And yet it occurred to me as I watched Jaws opening the trunk for us that he had no thought for the German at such times, that his strength was his happiness—yes, he was *happy* in himself as he did this; and if the German fired him it would make no difference; he could take the German's face in his hands when he got his pink slip and slowly squeeze it with his palms, so happy, so happy when the skull burst and shattered, so happy that no consequences could touch him. . . . Unlike the soldier, he knew exactly what he was doing. Unlike the pusher, he was not restricted or defined by his allegiance. He had attained the blessing. He was the Good that I had waited for. And as I loaded the books from the trunk into my pack, as I put my arm around Jenny, leading her down the ramp into the sunlight, I prayed that Jaws would never crush me—but Whom was I praying to?—and I kept my worship secret, to be out of hearing of whatever God might be greater still.

GUY TREBAY

Dunes

The dunes are moving. You cannot see this exactly, but they are drifting, a subtle flow that scientists refer to as "waves of shifting sand." In some places the dunes are small and ridged. In others they rise to form a crustal lip. I have always imagined that dunes began at the tideline, but their foundations are deep in the inshore waters of the continental shelf. They are hillcrests. They are the visible peaks of a submarine desert called the ocean floor. They rise and subside, crest and erode, or are inundated by storm waves and washed away, obliterated.

The dunes are systems: their "vital area" includes the primary dune and all the active land behind it, the area where "significant vegetation" begins. The primary dune, whose leading edge is called a "toe," is the most active dune; that is, the dune most dynamically in the process of gaining sand, or of losing it to erosion by water and wind.

There are two men in the dunes on a cold spring morning.

"You come here a lot?"

"First time."

"Believe it or not, me too."

Both are lying.

"What do you do?" asks one. "I mean . . . "

"For a living? I'm in sales."
"No . . . "
"Oh."
"It's kind of cold, huh?"
Nothing.
"So. What are you into?"
"Whatever's fun."
The idea floats.
"You well hung?"
"Pretty much."
"You want to get into something?"
"Why not?"

Buttressing the primary dune are secondary dunes. When droughts or storms or hurricanes corrupt the primary dune, the secondary dunes absorb the physical forces. These dunes are blanketed with vegetation: trees and shrubs take root in the flat and low-lying sections behind the leading edge. The trees and shrubs are followed by parasitic vines. In the dunes that flank Field Six at Jones Beach State Park, honeysuckle threads through cedars and stunted pines and the rust-red pokers of sumac. Poison oak and ivy lace the paths and leave the unwary with anklets of rash. Rodents race through underbrush. You can hear the nervous skitter of their claws. Roseate terns peck through the reeds, protecting their hatch from rats. There are other creatures in the underbrush whose ecology has a more ephemeral quality. No one documents them or writes abstracts about their numbers. They are the men who prowl the beach in all seasons looking for sex.

Behind the foredune palisade is a wide sunken pathway where sound is muted, the sand white and pristine. At the rear edge of this walkway a slight rise gives onto a canted apron of land, covered with tall reeds, wedged against Ocean Parkway. Grass grows on the roadway verge. Wind blows sand over the grass and onto the roadway and blurs the clean blacktop edge.

Cut into the reeds behind the foredune is a network of informal trails. Their shapes meander, pounded flat by countless feet. They twist and reverse. They go nowhere. They dead-end. The doorways to these paths are in places less perceptible than a crack in a stage curtain. The paths are semi-secret. They run in mazes carpeted with dead vegetation and ambushing spikes of bent grasses and fragments of broken beer bottles and aluminum cans and shreds of plastic beaten into a patterned carpet of trash. This is where the dunewalkers go. "We are aware of it," a park official once told me, her voice tentative, then drooping and sad. "But . . . we try to allow people to enjoy the beach without too much interference."

The two young men, a blond and his blonder friend, had smooth Donatello bodies. They arrived early on summer beach mornings and walked to the east end, where they laid out their belongings and dropped some Quaaludes. They shook the pills from a film canister and downed them with gulps of orange juice, then meticulously spread their towels, wedging the corners into the sand. They massaged oil onto each other, doing the tops of their feet and the places between the toes. Downwind of them you caught whiffs of cheap coconut smell.

One wore his peroxided curls tied in a red bandanna. The other had a shaggy brush-cut. The leaner man spent his first half-hour doing sit-ups on a towel. When the sun got hot they both lay back motionless, not stirring except to change the tape in their boom box. At noon they stood and brushed sand from their bikinis. They trotted to the surf and dove in. The ringletted one swam with surprisingly strong strokes. The other splashed around. They returned to the towel and dried themselves, raked combs through their pale hair, put on sunglasses, and headed into the shade of the reed trails beyond the first dune.

I followed them once and lost my way in the slatted light of the high reeds. I retraced my steps and walked in circles until I stumbled upon this sight: two naked backs, a red bandanna, one blond bent over a log while the second mounted him from the rear.

The meager range of flora the dunes can sustain is as elegantly specialized and tenuous as the land itself. Tucked in the lee of the primary dune are barberry, reed grass, saltmeadow grass, cordgrass, a bottle-green rush called blackgrass, and fleshy, knuckled saltwort. At the leading edge of the dunes grows a grass whose Latin name is *Ammophila breviligulata.* The sand ridges are fringed with ammophila: it grows in sprouts as insubstantial-looking as the tufts on an old man's scalp. Ammophila is tough, though: it withstands sandblast, storm wind, salt spray, the inundating swells driven ashore by hurricanes. It thrives in a droughty and infertile medium. It grows vigorously where it would seem that nothing could grow. It roots by means of underground runners and spreads that way and not by seed. It secures the dunes and bastes together a landscape by catching and accreting the vagrant grains of sand. The wind and the ocean might consume the dunes if ammophila didn't claim them.

Field Six is little more than a parking lot at the eastern edge of Jones Beach State Park. The island it occupies is a dragged heelprint formed in the wake of the last glacial retreat, a fragment of a longer ribbon of sand barriers separating the Atlantic from the Great South Bay. Jones Beach lies at the southern limit of what geologists call a drowned coast: as the name would suggest, its fragility is extreme. To the east of Field Six the dunes incline from the surf in a gentle ramp. The primary dunes jut toward the ocean, harshly sculptured and ridged, scalloped by waves and wind into moguls or knobs. Their flanks are always littered with a confetti of shattered shells.

It is twenty-one degrees on a January afternoon. A fitful wind carries onshore from the ocean. The weather is not hospitable to humans. The beach is purging itself at this time of year. Nonetheless, it is evident that many people have recently been here. A huge timber is wedged at an angle to one of the rear dunes, washed ashore in a storm. From where, I wonder? What heaved it this far up? The dark wood forms the outer perimeter of a small cul-de-sac walled with banks of sand. Between the timber and the dune is a hollow. In the hollow two men lie face to face, fully clothed and making love.

There is a miniature-golf course at Jones Beach. There is a band shell. There are walled pools and bathing pavilions. The buildings themselves are constructed of Ohio sandstone, cedar, and red brick. The architectural motifs are Mayan and Art Deco. The road system centers on a water tower said to be modeled on the campanile in St. Mark's Square in Venice. It has always looked like a canine erection to me.

In this place, where the Atlantic ceaselessly worries and smoothes the shore, the master builder Robert Moses envisioned

Jones Beach State Park water tower.

a people's pleasure ground. With public money (and twenty thousand dollars borrowed from his mother), he had roads cut through the flat and then relatively unpopulous center of Long Island, and bridged the salt marshes of Zach's Bay to bring automobiles to an impermanent barrier of sand. Moses hired the architect Herbert Magoon to design a resort on land annexed from locals by eminent domain. The architecture of Jones Beach quotes Frank Lloyd Wright and the dour Amsterdam school and holds in dialogue the changeable sky and ocean, the low dunes and long horizon. It opened several months before the '29 Crash.

Money was spent at Jones Beach, and details lavished on building in ways that money alone can't always guarantee: the pavement inset with slate sea horses; the coppered cornices; the roofless bathhouses entered through a wide corridor of shade and set behind concrete-block screens that create an atmosphere of underwater purdah. From the beginning, a visit to this beach was seen as an event. The changing episode. The boardwalk procession. A millionaire's amenity open to the many.

Inside the bathhouse you see fathers and sons and young men and older men who undress and put on swimsuits and leave for the ocean or the saltwater pool. There is also another group that stays behind. These men drift through the aisles and by the communal showers, wrapped in towels or wearing nothing. The towels are often tented with their semi-erections. They eye each other in the showers and soap their penises lavishly to work up heft. In the days before the Long Island Parks Commission renovated the bathhouses to prevent the practice, they would follow one another into dressing rooms and masturbate, fuck, or kiss.

I used to arrive at Jones Beach before the sun was high. I caught the 7:35 train from New York and the connecting bus to Jones Beach at Freeport to beat the mainland traffic. Even in the early mornings I saw the old man. He was tall and had a rumpled face. He wore khaki shorts and carried a small duffel. I often saw him sitting in the semi-dark of a changing booth with the door propped open. I often saw someone enter the booth and close the door. After the Parks Commission removed the bathing booths and installed tiny lockers, the old man shifted his activity to the dunes. When I last saw him there, he was genuflecting in front of a young man. The young man had his trunks tugged to his thighs, revealing two color zones of skin: brown at the stomach and white on the buttocks and hips. The young man kept his eyes closed, and seemed unsure of where to place his hands, whether to rest them on the old man's shoulders or grasp the old man's head. Finally, he crossed his arms in an attitude of nonchalance.

Between the bathing pavilions and the ocean are the ribboning miles of boardwalk; stands of mugho pine; carpet-beds of electric-blue ageratum and flame-tipped salvia; white-painted lifeguard shacks and scabbed white lifeguard chairs; and the strip of sand that at midday is too hot to walk across with bare feet. And there is the cooler surfside sand that is filled in summer with human caviar. In aerial beach photographs that the tabloids publish each summer, this scene would be captioned: "A REAL SCORCHER." The humans in these pictures are an indefinable mass.

But at ground level things are clearer. You can diagram the human strata and find that people are arranged in distinct territories established each hot summer morning and gone by dusk. To the north, near the level sand by the public buildings and outdoor grills, is a place where urban families camp. They bring radios, webbed sand-chairs, net bags filled with Pringle's potato chips and Kraft barbecue sauce and shrink-wrapped packs of chicken wings from El Guapo in the Bronx. Alongside the parking lot is a separate ground of older people who cling to the concrete curb and the scorching white sand at its edge. From their vantage the ocean is no more than a distant band of blue.

As you walk south toward the water, the territorial axis shifts. Radiating from the main lifeguard stand are groups of Latinos and blacks, of old people cautiously swathed or else heedlessly exposing their leather to further rays. There are groups of teenagers from South Shore towns. Irish or Italian or Jewish, mainly, they seem poised at a biological moment of beauty that starts with the first pubic fuzz and ends with the onset of ankle bracelets and tattoos. The teenagers cluster on blankets. They mist their skins with mineral water and listen to their radios while their gutty and affable elders plant striped sun umbrellas in the sand, play poker, dip into Igloo coolers of beer. The daddies guzzle and bloat their bladders. Then they announce a dip: "I'm going in to warm up the water."

North of this place is a desolate intermediate zone marked off with trash cans, and an area of isolated bathers who seem as unconnected to one another or to anything else as the driftwood stranded by the receding tide. Here the peaked foredune and a ridge of secondary dune form a portal and a hollow. Between the two dunes onshore winds die down, as if the air had been sucked away. Near here, in another season, I saw a couple copulate in a nest of blankets. They moved slowly, as if they weren't moving at all. Where they lay half-covered they were open to anyone's view. The fact that, from my own towel, I could observe them may have added to their excitement. By propping my chin on folded arms I could see them press spoonwise and shut their eyes pretending to sleep. I could see them begin a rhythm almost painfully slow. I could see a black-backed gull planing above the two. I flicked my gaze from them to the gull until I grew bored and drifted off. When I woke, the beach grass was creased and the sand empty in the place where the lovers had been.

The border to this area is marked by a kite-flying zone. I once saw a family of Muslims here averting their eyes as a stranger drifted by bare-breasted, trailing a scarf in the wind. I once saw two men here wearing wrestler's jerseys as swimsuits and imitating Ziegfeld girls. I once saw a man here whose beach companion was a life-size inflatable doll. "This is Mamie," he announced to the air. Mamie had been in swimming. He combed Mamie's hair and patted seawater from her rubber face and said tenderly, "Mamie smoked a little too much wacky weed today and almost drowned. Didn't she, Mamie?" He took Mamie back into the surf. From the shore, I could see her head bobbing, her red mouth open in helpless surprise. Later, I watched him drag Mamie up the beach and park her deflated figure on a dune.

And once, on an unseasonably mild February afternoon, I saw a man pull in to Field Six in a flame-red BMW sedan. He parked at an angle to the curb by the dunes. He pushed his car seat all the way back and reclined. He put on sunglasses and opened his fly. He shut his eyes and masturbated slowly. He ejaculated into his hand, then wiped himself off with a McDonald's napkin. He hit the electric window button, tossed the wad of damp paper onto the tarmac, and drove away.

Roosting not far from Field Six is the largest colony of roseate terns in the world. They inhabit the wetlands behind the secondary dune. Biologists study the terns and band them, chart their numbers, their migrating habits and viable eggs. They build them nests. But the terns ignore the man-made habitations, preferring to construct their own in tangles of storm fence flung down by late-winter storms. They breed well in their flimsy shelters. "Many birds can adapt to human visits to their colony on foot, provided that they are never molested," said a scientific report I read about these birds. "If visitors appear at regular times and follow prescribed routes around or through the colonies, many birds and mammals learn within a few seasons that the visitors present no danger and they will allow very close approach."

Park rangers and park police patrol the dunes in trucks. They erect wood barriers to deter foot traffic. They roll through the sand in vehicles with Cyclopean wheels. Ten years ago on the eastern part of Jones Beach, a sleeping couple was run over by a dump truck. The wheels rolled over their heads and pressed them deep into the sand. The couple survived. Of course, sleeping on the beach after dark is forbidden. Walking on the dunes is forbidden. Public nudity and sex are forbidden, too.

"Whereas the beach itself is tough, the dunes are fragile and any alteration of them by construction, removal of sand, removal of vegetation or traffic over them (even foot traffic) can lead to their demise." This observation, from the Planning Commission of Currituck County in the Outer Banks of North Carolina, appears in a clipping I've carried around for years. Attached to it is another clipping whose tautology appealed to me in some illogical way. "When both shifting and stable dunes are destroyed by man, there is nothing left to stabilize the remaining sea of drifting sand but man himself."

Outside the concession stand at Field Six I overheard this conversation:

"Have you been in the dunes yet?"

"Yeah."

"Meet anybody?"

"Yeah."

"What did he look like?"

"That, uh, weird kind of face. I mean, the ugliest kind of face. You know?"

"And the body?"

"A bodybuilder."

"And?"

"And what?"

"- - - - - - - -"

"What can I say? A sand romance. It lasted two minutes, and for two minutes I was in love."

Evolving Patois

Down there where I'm gone, they wear no shoes,
Talk scarce, if any, read earth and moon,
Wear burlap patched with scraps of paper bags,
Boil muddy water tender, burn corn and beans:
I find them in the past—fogged-in. Then
I ride with daddy and Emery in the pickup
Out past the junkyard and dump to where
The murderer stands on the porch unbreeching
His gun. Behind him the ancient dogtrot
Is caving in. He points at who is seeping
Blood into the sheet on the yard. He does
Not talk, though now's an hour before
The sheriff will come, and now tongue-
Tied Emery drones last week at the sale-barn,
"Yanver gek dat halfer, Banny Doe?" In my dream
The sheriff never comes. We shush the murder
Up and learn to gum the mush that daddy loved.
Each morning sun cuts through the dogtrot
And blasts the engine hanging from the tree,
And Emery rattles bolts, that genius of grease.
"Banny Doe, da toick convuda ih aw fuh up."

Mother of God, what more is there to say?
The troubles that women start are men.
But Emery is dead. Billy Joe dead in prison.
Twenty-seven years, the brain stutters
And slings a glib American macaroni: the sporting
Schlock of Joe Garagiola usurping

The more exorbitant voice of Alastair Cooke
In nearly everybody's head—and the South
Is history. It drawls from the graveyard:
A Dolly Parton whang, throw in the blunt
Excuse me almost nonexistent consonants
Of a drunk Brando doing Martin King.
One thing my daddy always like to say,
"Plan to make friends or money, don't offend."
But men may hear a little after they die—
Surely the dead are due some small politeness.

WILLIAM EGGLESTON

Los Alamos

a fragment

For the late
Dr. Thomas C. Boring
of Greenwood, Mississippi

A B C D E F G H J K
1 2 3 4 5 6 7 8 9 10

DIXIE
HAMBURGERS
HENRY T.
Smith
OVEN
Controls

JAX

While driving through New Mexico in 1973, William Eggleston stopped at Los Alamos, the forested site of the atomic bomb's clandestine development. He chose *Los Alamos* as the title for a sprawling body of work, then nearing completion: approximately twenty-two hundred images photographed between 1967 and 1974. This title, which cloaks his ostensible subjects, found in a vast American terrain, acknowledges with some irony Eggleston's belief in the aesthetic consequences of his private quest.

While Eggleston has extended the straightforward photographic tradition of such artists as Henri Cartier-Bresson, Walker Evans, and Robert Frank, he has also introduced and emphasized two crucial aesthetic considerations. Eggleston's virtually exclusive use of uninflected color photography was unprecedented, as was his emphatic rejection of prevailing conventions of worthy subject matter. These conventions became for Eggleston "the obvious," and he began to regard anything and everything he looked at as potentially compelling. He has recently declared, "I am at war with the obvious."

The photographs that make up *Los Alamos* include the center of Eggleston's world—Memphis and the Mississippi Delta—and trace his travels west from New Orleans to southern California and Las Vegas. Eggleston remarked in 1970 that the lengthy span of images generated from these travels was, for him, something like a fragment of a novel—a sympathetic viewer could not avoid bringing some narrative order, however disjunctive, to the sequence. This aesthetic intent parallels that in Eggleston's recently published *The Democratic Forest,* for which *Los Alamos* is the seminal precursor.

The eight images selected for this portfolio, while representative, must be seen as a fragmentary glimpse of the entirety of *Los Alamos.* Eggleston's original intention, as yet unrealized, was to produce an encyclopedic set of bound volumes containing original prints and no text. This major, early body of work has remained unpublished and largely unseen until this occasion.

—Walter Hopps

GEORGE STARBUCK

CARGO CULT OF THE SOLSTICE AT HADRIAN'S WALL

(December 1988)

OTinyBombOTiny
BombWhatGangof
MadmenMadeThee

OMiddleeastern
MasterpieceNoT
NTBetrayedThee

OEensieWeensie
IndyCarOCreamy
HalvahCandyBar

SeeEvenMrMovie
StarMakesFaces
ToDissuadeThee

IfEldAcquaints
TheElderlyWith
Frailty&Terror

ThePresidentOf
MegabucksFinds
Payable2Bearer

LiningsInLifes
Overcoats&Anti
DagoAnecdotes&

SummersBunchOf
HadjiiotesJust
HaddaBeAnError

OCheerfulnessO
WholesomenessO
AmityONiceness

OInfoInHisGrip
AttainingRegal
Impreciseness*

HeTakesTheCake
ForKindnessYet
290PersiansGet

NotOneSpasmNot
OneWetTremorOf
Thinktwiceness

* This form is recommended for beginners. It is as simple as it looks. Fourteen characters to a line. Difficulty arises only when a footnote is required. Then the poet must contrive a thirteen-character line in place of the canonical fourteener, so as to leave room for the asterisk. Most poems in the form evade the difficulty by doing without footnotes, save for poems like this which are designed to be put in textbooks.

SPEEDREADER SOLVESNOVEL

•

•

•

•

•

PoetsOughtaUse
WhatTheProsUse
GreatBigGeorge
EliotStanzasof
AlphabetBlocks
LikeBeesInABox
LikeRorschachs
FromACollected
JamesOrJoyceOr
CaryIMeanCarol
OatesPageAfter
PageTheSameDad
BlameAvalanche
IntoTheInkwell

(Directions: Connect wires; depress title.)

The World and Other Places

When I was a boy, I made model airplanes. We didn't have the money to go anywhere; sometimes we didn't have the money to go to the shop. There were six of us at night in the living room, six people and six carpet tiles. Usually the tiles were laid two by three in a dismal rectangle, but on Saturday, Airplane Night, we took one each and sat cross-legged with all the expectation of an Arabian prince. We were going to fly away—and we held on to the greasy underside of our mats, waiting for the magic word to lift us. Bombay, Cairo, Paris, Chicago: we took it in turns to say the word, and the one whose turn it was took my model airplane and spun it where it hung from the ceiling, round and round our huge blow-up globe. We'd saved cereal tokens for the globe, and it had been punctured twice. Iceland was covered in cellotape, and Great Britain was only a rubber bicycle patch on the panoply of the world.

I had memorized all the flight times from London Heathrow to anywhere you could mention. It was my job to announce them and to wish the passengers a pleasant flight. Sometimes I pointed out landmarks on the way, and we would lean over into the fireplace and have a look at Mont Blanc or crane our necks round the back of the sofa just to get a glimpse of the Rockies.

About halfway through our trip, Mum, who was Chief Steward, swayed down the aisle with cups of tea and toast and Marmite. After that, Dad came forward with next week's jobs around the house written on bits of paper and put in a hat. We took out our share, and somebody, the lucky one, would just get "Duty Free" on theirs and they didn't have to do a thing.

When we reached our destination, we were glad to get up and stretch our legs, and then my sister gave us each a blindfold. We put it on and sat quietly while one of us started talking about this strange place we were visiting . . .

How hot it is getting off the plane. Hot and stale like opening the door of a tumble dryer. There are no lights to show us where to go. Death will be this way. A rough passage with people we have never met and a hasty run across the tarmac to the terminal building. Inside, in the day-for-night illumination, a group of Indians are playing the cello. Where are they from, these orchestral refugees? Can it be part of the service? Beyond them, urchins in bare feet leap up and down with ragged cardboard signs, each bearing the name of someone more important than us. These are the people who will be whisked away in closed cars to comfortable beds. The rest of us will get on the bus.

Luggage. Heaven or Hell in the afterlife will be luggage or the lack of it. The virtuous ones, the ones who knew that love is enough and that possessions are only pastimes, will float free through the exit sign, their arms ready to hug their friends, their toothbrush in their pocket. The greedy ones, who stayed up late gathering and gathering like demented bees, will find that you can take it with you. The joke is that you have to carry it yourself.

Here's the bus. It has three, maybe four wheels, and the only part noisier than the engine is the horn. All human life is here. There is something to be said for not being in a closed car. I am traveling between a crate of chickens and a fortune-teller. The chickens peck at my leg and the fortune-teller suddenly grabs my palm. She laughs in my face. "When you grow up, you'll learn to fly."

For the rest of the journey I am bitten by midges.

At last we have reached the Hotel Cockroach. Dusty mats

cover the mud floor and the clerk on reception has an open wound in his cheek. He tells me he was stabbed but I am not to worry. Then he gives me some lukewarm tea and shows me my room. It has a view over the incinerator and is farthest from the bathroom. At least I will not learn to think highly of myself.

In the darkness and the silence I can hear, far below, the matter of life going on without me. The night shift. What are they doing, the people who come and go? What are their lives? Whom do they love, and why? What will they eat? Where will they sleep? How many of them will see the morning? Will I?

Dreams. The smell of incense and frangipani. The moon sailing on her back makes white passages on a dun-colored floor. The moon and the clouds white at the window. How many times have I seen it? How many times do I stop and look as though I've never seen it before? Perhaps it's true that every day is the world made new again but for our habits of mind. Frozen in thought, fossilized in what we have built, how dark is the tundra of our soul. During the night a mouse gives birth behind the skirting board.

At the end of the story, my family and I swapped anecdotes and exchanged souvenirs. Later we retired to bed with all the weariness of a traveler's reunion. We had done what the astronauts do: belted the world in a few hours and still found breath to talk about it.

I knew I would get away, better myself. Not because I despised who I was, but because I didn't know who I was. I was waiting to be invented.

We went up in an airplane, the pilot and I. It was a Cessna, modern and beautiful, off-white with a blue stripe right round it and a nose as finely balanced as a pedigree muzzle. I wanted to cup it in both hands and say, "Well done, boy."

In spite of the air-conditioned cockpit, overwarm and muzzy in an unexpected economy-class way, the pilot had a battered flying jacket stuffed behind his seat. It was a real one, grubby sheepskin and a steel zip. I asked him why he bothered. "Romance," he said. "Flying is romantic. Even now, even so."

We were under a 747 at the time and I thought of its orange

seats crammed three abreast on either side and all the odds and ends of families struggling with their beach mats and headphones. "Is that romantic?" I said, pointing upward.

He glanced out of the window. "That's not flying. That's following the road."

For a while we continued in silence. He didn't look at me, but sometimes I looked at him: strong jaw with a bit of stubble, brown eyes that never left the sky. He was pretending to be the only man in the air. His dream was the first dream when men in plus fours and motorcycle goggles pedaled with all the single-mindedness of a circus chimp to get their wooden frames and canvas wings upward and upward and upward. It was a solo experience, even when there were two of you. What did Amy Johnson say? "If the whole world were flying beside me, I would still be flying alone." Rhetoric, you think. Frontier talk. Then you reach your own frontier and it's not rhetoric anymore.

My parents were so proud of me when I joined the air force. I stood in our cluttered living room in my new uniform and I felt like an angel on a visit. I felt like Gabriel coming to tell the shepherds the good news.

"Soon you'll have your wings," said my mother, and my father got out the scotch.

In my bedroom, the model airplanes had been dusted. Sopwith Camel, Spitfire, Tiger Moth. I picked them up one by one and turned over their balsa-wood frames and rice-paper wings. I never used a kit. What hopes they carried! More than the altar at church, more than a good school report. In the secret places—under the fuselage, stuck to the tail fin—I had hidden my hopes.

My mother came in. "You won't be taking them with you?"

I shook my head. I'd be laughed at, made fun of. And yet each of us in our silent bunks at lights-out would be thinking of model airplanes and the things at home we couldn't talk about anymore.

She said, "I gave them a wipe anyway."

Bombay. Cairo. Paris. Chicago. I've been to those places now. I've been almost everywhere, and the curious thing is that after a while they begin to look the same. I don't mean the buildings or the scenery, I mean the people. We're all preoccupied with the same things: how to live, whom to love, and where we go when it's over. Pressing needs—the need to eat, the need to make money, both forcing the same hungry expression into the face—sometimes distract us from our mortality. Those needs met, however temporarily, we can't stop ourselves reviewing again and again how short is the space between day and night.

I saw three things that made this clear to me.

The first was a beggar in New York. He was sitting, feet apart, head in hands, on a low wall outside an all-night garage. As I went past him he whispered, "Do you have two dollars?"

I got out the change and gave it to him. He said, "Will you sit with me a minute?"

His name was Bill, and he was a compulsive gambler trying to go straight. He thought he might get a job on Monday morning if only he could have two nights in a hostel to sleep well and keep clean. For a week he had been sleeping by the steam duct of the garage. I gave him the hostel money and some extra for food, and the clenched fist of his body unfolded. He was talkative, gentle. Already, in his mind, he had the job and was making a success of it and had met a sweet woman in a snack bar. He got up to hurry over to the hostel before it closed. He shook my hand. "You know, the worst thing about being on the street, it's not that you're hungry and cold, it's that nobody sees you. They don't look at you, or they look through you. It's like being a ghost. If you're already dead, what's the point of trying to live?"

The second was a dress designer I met in Milan. She was at the very top of her profession, and she worked long after the others had gone home. Anyone passing could see the light in her window. It was the only one. I never had time to talk to her over a meal or even a cup of coffee. She had food brought into her studio, and she ate like an urchin, pencil in one hand, in the other a palmful of olives. She spat the stones at her models.

"I never take holidays," she said. "My models, they are always taking holidays. They don't care."

"Perhaps you should rest," I said. "Go to one of your houses." She had five houses, but she lived in a rented flat above her studio.

"And what would I do all day, Mr. Pilot? Stare at the sky?" She went to her worktable and picked up a pair of shears. "You start thinking, you cut your own throat. What is there to think about? I've tried it, and it ends up the same way. In your mind there is a bolted door. You spend your life trying to avoid that door. You go to parties, work hard, have babies, have lovers—it doesn't make any difference what way you choose. But when you are on your own, quiet, nothing to do, or sometimes just walking up the stairs, you see the door again, waiting for you. Then you have to hurry, you have to stop yourself pulling the bolt and turning the handle. On the other side of the door is a mirror, and you will see yourself for the first time. You will see what you are and, worse than that, what you are not."

The third was a woman in the park with her dog. The dog was young, the woman was old. She carried a shopping bag and every so often took out a bottle and a bowl and gave the dog a drink of water.

"Come on, Sandy," she'd say when he'd finished. Then she'd disappear into the bushes, the dog's tail bobbing behind.

She fascinated me because she was everything I'm not. Put us together, side by side, and what do we look like? I'm six feet tall, in an airman's uniform, and I have a strong grip and steady eyes. She's about five feet high and threadbare. I could lift her with one hand. But if she met my gaze, I'd drop my eyes and blush like a teenager. She's got the edge on me. She's not waiting to be invented; she's done it herself.

How do I know? I don't know, but increasingly I'm looking at people to see who's a fake and who's genuine. Most of us are fakes, surrounded by gilded toys and fat address books and important offices, anything to keep away from that bolted door.

For some years, the early years of my air force days, I stopped worrying about such questions. I was happy and adventurous and it was obvious that I was a man because I was doing a man's job. That's how we define ourselves, isn't it? Then one day I woke up with the curious sensation that I wasn't myself. I hadn't turned into a beetle or a werewolf. My friends treated me as they usually did. I put on my favorite well-worn clothes, bought newspapers and eggs, walked in the park. At last I went to see a doctor. I said, "Doctor, I'm not myself these days." He asked me about my sex life and gave me a course of antidepressants.

I went to the library and took out books from the philosophy and psychology sections. I read R. D. Laing, who urged me to make myself whole. Then Lacan, who wants me to accept that I'm not. And all the time I thought, "If this isn't me, then I must be somewhere." That's when I started traveling so much. I left the air force and bought my own plane. Mostly I teach; sometimes I take out families who've won the first prize in a soup-packet competition. It doesn't matter. I have plenty of free time and I do what I need to do, which is look for myself. I know that if I fly long enough, wide enough, and far enough, I'll get a signal that tells me there's another aircraft on my wing. I'll glance out of my window, and it won't be a friendly Red Devil. It'll be me I see in the cockpit of that other plane.

I went home to see my mother and father. I flew over their village, taxied down their road, and left the nose of my plane pushed up against their front door. The tail was just a little on the pavement, and I was worried that some traffic warden might give me a ticket for causing an obstruction. I hung a sign on the back saying "Flying Doctor."

I'm always nervous about going home, just as I'm nervous about rereading books that have meant a lot to me. My parents want me to tell them about the places I've been and what I've seen. Their eyes are eager and full of love. Bombay, Cairo, Paris, Chicago: we've invented them so many times that to tell the truth can only be a disappointment. The blow-up globe still hangs over the mantelpiece, its faded plastic crinkly and torn. The countries of the Common Market are held together by red tape.

We go through my postcards one by one, and I give them presents: a sari for my mother, a Stetson for my father. They are the children now. We have a cup of tea and at evening they come outside to wave me off. "It's a lovely plane," says my mother. "Does it give you much trouble?"

I rev the engine, and the neighbors stand astonished in their doorways as the plane gathers speed down on our quiet road. A moment before the muzzle breaks through the apostles' window in our little church, I take off, rising higher and higher and disappearing into a bank of cloud.

无 题

比事故更陌生
比废墟更完整

说出你的名字
它永远弃你而去

钟表内部
留下青春的水泥

Untitled

more unfamiliar than an accident
more complete than ruins

having uttered your name
it abandons you forever

youth's mud is left
inside the clock

Translated by Bonnie S. McDougall

无题

我看不见
清澈的水池里的金鱼
隐秘的生活
我穿越镜子的努力
没有成功

一匹马在古老的房顶
突然被勒住缰绳
我转过街角
乡村大道上的尘土
遮蔽天空

Untitled

I cannot see
the secret life
of the goldfish in the limpid pond
my efforts to pass through the mirror
have not succeeded

a horse on the ancient roof
is suddenly reined in
I turn the corner of the street
the dust on the village's main road
obscures the sky

Translated by Bonnie S. McDougall

LARRY FLYNT
FOR
PRESIDENT

Larry Flynt at Home

From interviews by Jean Stein

Good morning, I am your worst nightmare come true: a fabulously wealthy pornographer with the courage and willingness to spend his last dime to expose how you are perverting the Constitution of this great land. Now let's get down to business.

—"Larry Flynt for President"
campaign ad, Nov. 1983

Dennis Hopper
I decided I was going to blow myself up at the Big H Speedway—something I saw at the rodeo when I was a kid. They called it "the human stick of dynamite." I was convinced that somebody was trying to make a hit on me, and it would be easier to kill me if I was doing this. If I lived through it, then I was destined to live for a while. The stunt man who helped me put the thing together said, "You'll be disoriented for a few weeks." Little did he fucking know. A week later I was in Mexico and I really flipped out. I was on location for a film. They'd asked me to play the head of the DEA [Drug Enforcement Agency]. I thought it was just a plot and they were going to get me. Next thing I

knew I was walking through the jungle naked. I was convinced everybody understood everything I was thinking.

I ended up in Studio 12, where they took me to recover from the alcohol and drugs and so on. I got an offer from Larry Flynt to do the first celebrity shoot for *Hustler*. I was so out of it, I thought it was some sort of code. It sounded really interesting to me. So Flynt moved me into his house and I became like his top advisor. And here I was, just out of a fucking mental institution. I'd agree with anything he said. "Oh yeah, run for President, sure, why not? Wish I'd thought of it, Larry." In the beginning I thought he was kidding about running for President. Then he suddenly wasn't kidding. All these '60s radicals started showing up: Stokely Carmichael and, what's his name, Rap Brown would come in. And Russell Means would be downstairs. He was Larry's Vice Presidential candidate. And Terry and Leary and myself, just the most radical people.

Terry Southern

Den Hopper called me from Larry Flynt's: "I've sent you a first-class round-trip ticket and I want you to come out. I have a proposition for you. Take my word, it's a good thing. I'll meet the plane." And so I went out without knowing anything except that Den had recommended it.

Den did meet me at the airport and he said, "Man, you're going to dig this scene. This is fantastic!"

When we arrive, the iron gate swings open and they wave Den in. Here I am in this gigantic place, three blocks up from the Bel Air Hotel. I'm trying to think whose house it used to be—Janet Leigh and Tony Curtis, or Sonny and Cher, or somebody. Many generations of mismatched celebrities. There were tennis courts and pools on each side of the house with waterfalls and things like that. Well secured—it's patrolled by guys carrying Uzi machine guns. Three uniformed guards outside the fence, and then on the inside three huge bodybuilder types, dressed in white short-sleeves to show off their gigantic biceps. The guards say, "Larry and Althea are resting," which meant that they were just nodded out. So Den and I go up to these fantastic adjoining suites, like something out of the Bel Air Hotel.

Den had become friendly with Althea, who was Larry Flynt's

wife. A very curious girl from Georgia, extremely provincial, but with what you might call "keen native intelligence"—a sort of poor-white-trash Whoopi Goldberg. She was heavily into pleasure—obsessed with doing all kinds of things for pleasure—especially all kinds of dope. She had a voracious appetite, but she was an innocent—a babe in the woods without a conscience. In an effort to cool her out, Larry had asked her, "What would you like to do, baby? You name it." She said, "I want to make a movie about Jim Morrison." "All right, you've got it." She consults Den Hopper, and he says: "Well, the person you want to get to write the script is my friend Terry Southern." She said, "Oh, right, good idea." So Den tells me, "We'll write the script together. I already asked them for twenty-five thousand dollars apiece up front." And he hands me this envelope of hundred-dollar bills *that* thick: "Here, here's yours. I'll show you mine—see, they're the same." "Where should we keep it?" I asked. "I don't know, I'm keeping mine behind this book. The other day I got so stoned I couldn't remember which book it was. I tore the place apart."

Then we met this one particular guard who, it turns out, is also the chief drug procurer. He says, "Larry's trying to get Althea to clean up, so it's very important not to give her any dope." Then he tells Dennis, "Larry wants to see you in his study." And Den says to me, "I'll see you later. Why don't you just wander around?"

So I'm wandering around the halls and I turn the corner and there's this waiflike girl with wild eyes. She said, "Are you Terry?" I said yes. "Hi baby, I'm Althea," and while we were still having a hug she said, "Are you holding any dope?" When I said no, she said, "I'm surprised there's any friend of Dennis Hopper who isn't holding dope." I said, "Well, I'm not. I just got here and I haven't had a chance. Besides, a guy with a gun has already told me you're not to have any." She said, "Yes, they may tell you that, but they don't know what they're talking about. My doctor said I should have dope or I'm going to stress out."

She said, "I'm so glad that you're going to do the Jim Morrison thing. I'm in love with him. I think he's still alive, don't you?" "I don't know about that," I said, "but his spirit certainly lives on." "Nah," she said, "I mean, he's been seen by a lot of people. He was seen in Venice not long ago"—Venice, California, which is where he used to hang out. "Come downstairs, I want you to meet a friend of mine who's just got here." It was Tim Leary. He very surreptitiously passed her some dope. "Sunshine from the East," he said. "A CARE package from the East." I said, "What are you doing here?" He said, "I'm meeting Liddy. Liddy and I have been rehearsing here." G. Gordon Liddy and Leary were doing this "debating tour," and they rehearsed their debate at Flynt's. "I don't want to meet him," I said, "he represents everything bad." And Leary just beamed. "Oh, you'll like him," he said.

Timothy Leary
You can hate Liddy, but you've got to admire him. When they asked him if he swore "to tell the truth, the whole truth, so help me God," you know what Liddy said? "No." Liddy's political attitudes are Paleolithic—he's a cold warrior—but he's got a sense of humor. He has that spunky, cocky, little-guy attitude that Larry Flynt liked. Liddy was having a little trouble with his taxes, so Larry flew him out to be a consultant on security. It was just an excuse on Larry's part to help Gordon out.

Terry Southern
The next guy to arrive was Marjoe—you know, that guy who used to be a child evangelist. And the other person who was a permanent guest for the moment was Madalyn Murray. Madalyn Murray has devoted her entire life to trying to get the Bible outlawed in school. She's a professional atheist, very courageous. For some reason Larry Flynt was interested in her cause. I think he wanted to fuck her . . . mind-fuck her I mean.

> **Many of you have said, "I can agree with a great deal of Larry Flynt's philosophy, but not burning the American flag, or desecrating the American flag." More people have died over that rag than any other rag since the beginning of time.**
>
> **—Larry Flynt,**
> publisher's statement, *Rebel*, Dec. 1983

Terry Southern

About 4:00 P.M. Larry Flynt comes in and he says, "Sundowner time. Time for a sundowner." He's in a wheelchair. His wheelchair is motorized and gold-plated, and it has little American flags like on an ambassador's car. He's wearing this big diaper he had made up from an American flag. "They treat me like a baby," he said, "so I'm going to behave like one. And if I poo-poo in my diaper, I'll be poo-pooing on the American flag." He's trying to explain this to this huge Indian—what the hell is his name? He's a great Indian guy who's about seven feet tall . . . Means, Russell Means. He's there, and meanwhile I hear this shouting, and it sounds like a big argument, but it's just Liddy and Tim Leary rehearsing their act, I mean their "debate." About time for dinner, Frank Zappa arrives, you know him. Quite a grand zany. So there's this very long table of odd people.

After dinner Larry said, "Come into my study, Terry, you're going to need some money for the weekend." We went into his office and he said, "There's a briefcase right by the couch where you're sitting. Put it in your lap and open it." So I did. It was full of packs of hundred-dollar bills. Larry said, "It's a million dollars. I have to have this on hand to give validity to the offer." And he showed me this circular: *A standing offer from Larry Flynt to the following women who are prepared to show gyno-pink. One million cash to: Barbara Bach, Cathy Bach, Barbi Benton, Cheryl Tiegs. . . .* They were mostly kind of obscure, but there were one or two that were totally out of place, like Gloria Steinem and Jane Fonda. He was offering a million dollars if they'd pose and do a gyno spread, what he called "flashing pink." And so he said, "Take whatever you think you'll need for the weekend," and he made a point of turning around to use the phone so I could take what I wanted. When he finished his call, he asked, "How much did you take?"

"Two hundred dollars."

"You must be a fool—you could have taken more."

I said, "I don't think I need any more than that."

"Well, I like an honest man," he said. "Do you think Dennis Hopper's honest?"

"I know him well," I said. "He's very honest."

"Well, he claimed he lost the twenty-five thousand dollars," Larry said. "Do you believe that?"

"I think he found it again," I said. "Didn't he tell you?"

"Oh, that's right," he said, "he told me."

It must have been that night, I got a call about 3:00 A.M. "Terry? Althea. What are you holding?"

"I'm not holding anything."

"Dennis told me you were holding. I've got to have something, baby, I'm stressing out."

I said, "Well, let me speak with Dennis."

"I just spoke to him and he claims he doesn't have anything, but I don't believe him."

So I went to Dennis and I said, "Why did you pass her on to me?"

"Well, I don't know what to do about this," he said. "Here, I've got one joint, give her this."

"Why don't *you* give it to her?" I said.

"I'm not dressed."

"Well, if you think it's all right. . . ." So I went out in the hall, and sure enough, there she was, in a weird white lady-of-the-lake nightgown, and she rushes up, and I'm just about to give her the joint when I see this huge security guard, Hans is his name. Monstro-Kraut. She said, "Drop it down the front of my gown and he won't see it." I did, but it fell right through. She was a bit on the frail-knocker side. "It fell on the floor," I said. So she put her foot on it, she's standing on it.

Meanwhile Hans says, "Is there any trouble?"

"Oh no, just having a little stroll here, and bumped into Althea here." Meanwhile she's trying to pick up the joint with her toes, you know. I mean absurd.

He looks down and says, "Wait a minute, I'll help you."

"No, no," Althea said, "I don't need your help. When I need your help, I'll ask for it."

"All right, all right. Have it your way. But I know, I know." And so he turned and left.

The next day Larry Flynt sent for me. "Althea is in no condition to talk about her projects because somebody's been giving her drugs. Do you know anything about it?" "No," I said, "I don't know anything about it." "Hans said that he saw you passing her dope in the hall, passing it from your foot to her foot. He says that you keep your dope in your shoe. He says your shoe is your stash." I said, "Well, Dennis Hopper's going to have to explain all of this." Meanwhile, as a joke, I had written on a piece of paper right above Dennis's bed: "Rise and shine, Hopper, we've got some tooting to do!"

Larry Flynt couldn't function from the waist down. As long as he kept certain nerves alive, he had a theoretical chance of regaining the use of his limbs. Finally the pain got so bad that he was advised to have this operation whereby they severed these nerves. But during this period the pain was terrific, so he actually had a prescription for morphine and had developed quite a little oil-burner of a habit. Althea was constantly plotting to steal it from him. So Flynt decided to put a permanent guard on his stash of M. He had tried to hide it every night, like Dennis hid his twenty-five thou, but he would forget where he'd hid it. He had periods of great lucidity and then periods where he wouldn't know what was going on.

LFP inc.

INTEROFFICE

To: **All Employees**
From: **Larry Flynt**
Date: **September 29, 1983**
Re: **DRUG USE**

I am aware that the use of drugs, especially cocaine, is widespread within this company.

I am giving each of you an opportunity to stop doing drugs. The company will cover the expense of treatment for anyone who wants to be helped.

If you don't seek help and I find out that you are using drugs, you will be terminated immediately, regardless of what your position is.

Terry Southern

Meanwhile, the Jim Morrison project was in a shambles. Nobody had bothered to look into anything like the rights. I told Althea, "Well, we're having a little problem with the rights. You have a few lawyers, I understand. Could we put one of them on trying to sort out the rights to this story? We're going to have to get an agreement from each of the Doors, or else we can't use the name 'Jim Morrison,' we can't use the music." She looked so despondent that I felt obliged to come up with something. "Maybe we could do it in such a way that everyone would know it's really about Morrison," and she said, "Oh yeah, I can dig it, I can dig it. It might be interesting to do it that way."

Althea was the producer and she wanted to meet some movie stars. She said, "Let's have a party and get some P.R. going for the Jim Morrison project. Now I want you and Dennis to make up a list of all the movie stars you can think of and invite them to the party." And Larry wanted to publicize his million-dollar offer for celeb-pink, so he wanted the attaché case full of cash there for the photographers and journalists to feel and photograph. At first Althea said, "I think that's going to cheapen the Jim Morrison Story aspect of it," but Larry said, "No, it won't. A million dollars cash don't cheapen nothin', baby."

> **If elected, my primary goal will be to eliminate sexual ignorance and venereal disease. Every ounce of strength I can muster, both physically and psychologically, will be used courageously and endlessly to remove the massive repressive hand of government, the ruling class, from the crotch of the American people.**
>
> **— Larry Flynt,**
> presidential candidacy announcement, Oct. 16, 1983

Terry Southern

Dennis and I were there about three weeks. He did his shoot for the *Hustler* series called "Celebrity Porn" where a movie actor is invited to set up an erotic storyboard. Den, being a poet of the lens, shot it himself. He created a gallerylike situation with some paintings he had done, and then he had these girls posing on a couple of settees. Two girls doing lez-type lovemaking, with some of his paintings in the background. So it served his sort of aesthetic purpose. And a big photograph of him. I was there for part of the shoot. Hot stuff at first, then it got too predictable.

Dennis Hopper

I'd made a precedent: I established that this simulated sex was OK, but not in my pictures. It was going to be real. So if they were going to send me women who weren't really interested in doing it, I wasn't interested. They sent me in about ten women. I'd get them in the room, and they'd take off their clothes and they'd say, "But we only do simulated sex." Finally Flynt had them bring in the guy who'd been sending the girls over, and the security guard starts hitting him with a stick and pounding him. Then he takes out a .45 and says he's going to shoot him if he tries to run. And Flynt is yelling and screaming. Terry wouldn't look, he didn't want to see it. I was watching. "Nothing's happening," I said, "he's just yelling at him." But it was really weird, it was awful.

Then you start thinking, "How do I get out of here?" I'm living in this house like a monk. Sex must be going on everywhere, but none for me. And Terry and I were sitting there like angels. I swear to God, it's true. I guess we were just the weirdos upstairs. Every time we'd come down, we'd get bodyguards.

> **Fuck this court! You deprive me of the counsel of my choice! Goddamn motherfuckers! You're nothing but nine assholes and a cunt!**
>
> **—Larry Flynt**
> to the U.S. Supreme Court, Nov. 9, 1983

Dennis Hopper

I got up one morning and turned on the television, and I swear to God they said, "The Flynt house is surrounded." It's all over the news media that we're surrounded by Feds! There are helicopters everywhere. They were after the tapes. Flynt had gotten the DeLorean and Alfred Bloomingdale tapes, and Reagan tapes supposedly. He had made a statement that he was going to shoot the first Fed to enter the gates right through the throat—not between the eyes but in the throat, where they suck cock, or some bullshit.

I got dressed quickly. I went downstairs and found one of Flynt's bodyguards, a guy who'd been a Green Beret in Vietnam, a killer, a stone fucking killer. I said to him, "Is there anything I can do?" "Yeah. Put this grenade in your mouth and run the wall. Or go back to your room." I said, "Yeah, well I'm back in the room. Anything you need, I'll be up there."

I went to the room, tried to calm myself down, did some more cocaine. Terry was stoned or asleep. I finally got him half-awake. "Oh, it'll be lunch at the Beverly Hills Hotel," he says to me. "We may not be alive!" I screamed. He went back to sleep.

> **So move over motherfuckers! This is not the Last Supper. This is the morning after and I am the main man. I hope you don't think I have shown contempt for the Court. I have done my damnedest to conceal it.**
>
> **—"Larry Flynt for President"**
> campaign ad, Nov. 1983

Timothy Leary
At the time, Larry was being fined like ten thousand dollars a day for contempt of court—withholding the source of the DeLorean tapes. One day he hired a bus, and he had twenty street hustlers from the Sunset Strip, all the young ladies in high heels, pay back the fine in wheelbarrows filled with pennies. It was all being taped and filmed. And then Larry was dragged off to Terminal Island.

Dennis Hopper
I got this part to play this CIA guy in Sweden, so I left. Larry went to prison. Althea came in and destroyed the metal detector

at the Federal prison in Missouri. So she was put in prison. And then I never saw any of them again.

> **After all is said and done, who would you prefer as your next President? A Hollywood ham, an addle-brained astronaut, or a smut peddler who cares?**
>
> **—Larry Flynt,**
> presidential candidacy announcement, Oct. 16, 1983

ABOUT THE COVER

With this issue, *Grand Street* initiates a new approach to its cover: an actual-size detail of a chosen artwork is featured. On the page to the right, the entire work is reproduced. An enlarged detail from the same work appears on the title page. This graphic format will be an ongoing feature of *Grand Street*, with a different artist selected for each issue.

Saul Steinberg's image of the artist, inventing himself from his materials, feverishly at work, and, in Steinberg's words, "just slightly insane," seemed appropriate as a cover for a journal of *Grand Street*'s persuasion.

In this instance, the cover artist, Saul Steinberg, is featured elsewhere in the issue with a portfolio of recent work.

—Walter Hopps

Saul Steinberg
Untitled, 1964
Ink on paper
11 x 14⅝ in.
Courtesy of the artist

CONTRIBUTORS

John Ashbery's most recent collection of poems is *April Galleons* (Viking-Penguin, 1987).

Bei Dao was coeditor of *Today*, an underground publication of the 1978 Democracy Movement in China, and initiated an open letter to the Chinese authorities in 1989, asking for the release of political prisoners. He now lives in exile in West Berlin. New Directions has published two volumes of his work, *The August Sleepwalker* (poetry) and *Waves* (fiction).

Elizabeth Bishop (1911–1979) was called "our greatest national treasure" by the poet James Merrill. Her *Complete Poems: 1927–1979* appeared in 1983 and her *Collected Prose* in 1984; both were published by Farrar, Straus & Giroux.

Moira Brown is an artist who lives and works in New York and Key West.

Sandra Cisneros is the author of *My Wicked Wicked Ways* and the award-winning *The House on Mango Street.* This story is from a collection to be published next spring by Random House. Cisneros currently lives in central Texas.

Anne Doran was born in Canada in 1957. She lives and works in New York City, where she has had several solo exhibitions. Her work has been included in shows at the Centre Pompidou in Paris and the Stedelijk Museum in Amsterdam.

William Eggleston is based in Memphis, Tennessee. His recent book *The Democratic Forest* has been hailed as one of the finest achievements in color photography. Other publications include *William Eggleston's Guide, Graceland,* and *Morals of Vision.*

Robert Giroux, a partner at Farrar, Straus & Giroux, has edited and introduced the posthumous prose collections of John Berryman, Elizabeth Bishop, and Robert Lowell. He is author of *The Book Known as Q,* a study of Shakespeare's sonnets, and

A Deed of Death, about the unsolved murder of movie director W. D. Taylor.

Joy Harjo was born in Tulsa, Oklahoma, in 1951 and is an enrolled member of the Creek Tribe. Her most recent collection of poetry is *In Mad Love and War,* published by Wesleyan University Press. She is also the author of *Secrets From the Center of the World* and *She Had Some Horses.* She lives in Tucson, Arizona, where she plays saxophone in her own band.

Dennis Hopper's movies include *Easy Rider* and *Blue Velvet.* An exhibition of his photographs is currently touring Japan, and he has just finished directing his sixth major feature, *Hot Spot.* He notes: "After the period described in 'Larry Flynt at Home,' I went into rehab and have six years' sobriety—drug- and alcohol-free. This may sound like a Terry Southern fantasy, but unfortunately it's all true."

Walter Hopps, an art historian and curator with the Menil Foundation, served as founding director of its new museum in Houston. His previous exhibitions have included *Joseph Cornell, Marcel Duchamp,* and *Robert Rauschenberg.* A forthcoming exhibition is *Max Ernst: Dada and the Dawn of Surrealism.*

Matt Jasper: pilot, ice-hockey arena owner-operator, burglar alarm and electronic-intrusion-device specialist, sports shop manager, automobile salesman. He's reported to be extremely outgoing and personable.

Rodney Jones lives in Carbondale, Illinois, where he teaches at Southern Illinois University. His most recent book, *Transparent Gestures,* published in 1989 by Houghton Mifflin, won this year's National Book Critics Circle Award in poetry.

Li-Young Lee's second book, *The City in Which I Love You* (BOA Editions), is the 1990 Lamont Poetry Selection. He has received a Whiting Writer's Award, a grant from the National Endowment for the Arts, and a Guggenheim Fellowship; his first book, *Rose* (BOA Editions), won the Delmore Schwartz Memorial Award.

Olivier Messiaen was born in Avignon, France, in 1908. He is Professor of Composition at the Conservatoire de Paris and a member of the Institut de France.

Les Murray lives in hilly cattle country two hundred miles north of Sydney, Australia. Two collections of his poetry have been published by Persea Books, and his collected poems are forthcoming from Farrar, Straus & Giroux next year.

Tom Paulin edited *The Faber Book of Political Verse. Seize the Fire,* his version of *Prometheus Bound,* has recently been published by Faber & Faber.

Edward Said is professor of English and Comparative Literature at Columbia and the author of *Orientalism* and *The World, the Text, and the Critic.* His book *Musical Elaborations* (Columbia University Press) will be published in the spring of 1991.

Terry Southern's novels include *Flash and Filigree, The Magic Christian, Candy* (with Mason Hoffenberg), and *Blue Movie.* His screenplays include *Barbarella, Dr. Strangelove, Easy Rider,* and *The Magic Christian.* Southern has just completed his fifth novel, *A Texas Summer.* A collection of short fiction, *Red-Dirt Marijuana,* has just been reissued by Citadel Underground Press.

George Starbuck, professor emeritus of English at Boston University, now makes his home in Tuscaloosa. His eight books include *Bone Thoughts, White Paper, The Argot Merchant Disaster,* and *Richard the Third in a Fourth of a Second.*

Jean Stein's forthcoming book, from which "Larry Flynt at Home" is an excerpt, will be published by Farrar, Straus & Giroux.

Saul Steinberg lives in Manhattan and Amagansett, Long Island. *Canal Street,* a collaboration with Ian Frazier, will be published this fall as part of the Whitney Museum's Artists and Writers Series. Steinberg is represented by The Pace Gallery in New York.

Antonio Tabucchi was born in Pisa in 1943. He is professor of Portuguese Literature at the University of Genoa. His books include *Piazza d'Italia, Il piccolo naviglio, Notturno indiano,* and *Il filo dell'orizzonte.* "Past Composed" is from *I volatili del Beato Angelico,* to be published in translation by Chatto & Windus in May 1991.

Lewis Thomas is scholar-in-residence at the Cornell University Medical College and president emeritus of Memorial Sloan Kettering Cancer Center. His books include *The Lives of a Cell* and *Late Night Thoughts on Listening to Mahler's Ninth Symphony.* "The World at a Glance" will appear in Doubleday's anthology *Living Philosophies,* and in Thomas's next book, *Et Cetera, Et Cetera,* to be published in 1991 by Little, Brown.

Guy Trebay writes a weekly column for *The Village Voice.* He has contributed to numerous publications, among them *Harper's* and *The New Yorker.*

William T. Vollmann is the author of *You Bright and Risen Angels, The Rainbow Stories,* and *The Ice-Shirt.* "Divine Men" is taken from a collection entitled *Thirteen Stories and Thirteen Epitaphs.*

Jeanette Winterson was born in Lancashire, England, in 1959. Her first novel, *Oranges Are Not the Only Fruit,* won the Whitbread and John Llewellyn Rhys prizes. Her most recent book is *Sexing the Cherry.*

ILLUSTRATIONS

cover & title page Saul Steinberg, untitled (details), 1964, ink on paper, 11 x 14⅝ in. Courtesy of the artist.

pp. 10, 20 Cisneros family photographs, c. 1950s. Courtesy of Sandra Cisneros.

p. 26 Alberto Giacometti, *Jean Genet,* 1955, oil on canvas, 25 x 21 in. Tate Gallery, London. Courtesy of Art Resource.

pp. 52, 56, 63 Postcards, c. 1900. Courtesy of Saul Steinberg.

pp. 53, 57, 62 Saul Steinberg, untitled (details), 1988, xerographic enlargements with pencil and oilstick. Courtesy of the artist.

pp. 54–55, 58–61 Saul Steinberg; six drawings; 1988; charcoal, pastel, and oilstick on paper; 18 x 24 in. each. Courtesy of The Pace Gallery, New York.

p. 70 Frank Martin, *Force. Lifeforce* (detail), 1989, handmade photographic image, gelatin silver print, 50 x 65 in. Courtesy of the artist.

p. 80 Toy typewriter, c. 1935. Photograph by Don Quaintance.

p. 88 Elizabeth Bishop, manuscript page, c. 1934. Courtesy of Vassar College Library.

p. 90 Elizabeth Bishop, untitled, n.d., pencil on hotel stationery, 6½ x 5¼ in. Courtesy of Vassar College Library.

pp. 110, 112–18 Reprinted, by permission of the publisher, from Olivier Messiaen, *Saint François d'Assise* (Paris: Alphonse Leduc), 164–70.

p. 122 Book cover with fifteenth-century prayer book illumination. Courtesy of Sellerio editore Palermo. Photograph by Ken Cohen.

p. 132 William T. Vollmann and Moira Brown; four pages from *Divine Men* (New York: Cotangent Press, 1989, edition of 13); linoleum cut, ink and paint on paper. Courtesy of the artists.

pp. 138, 143 Courtesy of New York State Office of Parks, Recreation and Historic Preservation–Long Island Region.

pp. 153–60 William Eggleston, eight untitled photographs, 1967–72 variously, Ektacolor prints from 35mm color negatives, 11 x 14 in. each. Courtesy of the artist.

p. 164 Vintage line-cut illustrations.

p. 176 Anne Doran, untitled, 1990, cut photographs on paper, 17 x 21 in. Courtesy of the artist.

p. 204 Maullo(?), untitled, 1990, offset lithographic poster, 21 x 16 in. Street art (?) found in lower Manhattan.

Perfect Vision

"A haunting and unnerving experience . . . Oates recalls Henry James in her ability to explore not just surfaces and actions but connection of thoughts and feelings."
—*Chicago Tribune.*
Also available on audio-cassette from Harper Audio.
$8.95

"Arresting family portraits, sepia-stained in their poignance and scope . . . Leavitt has an eloquent touch and a writer's heart."—*Boston Globe.* "One of his generation's most gifted writers."
—Michiko Kakutani, *New York Times.*
$8.95

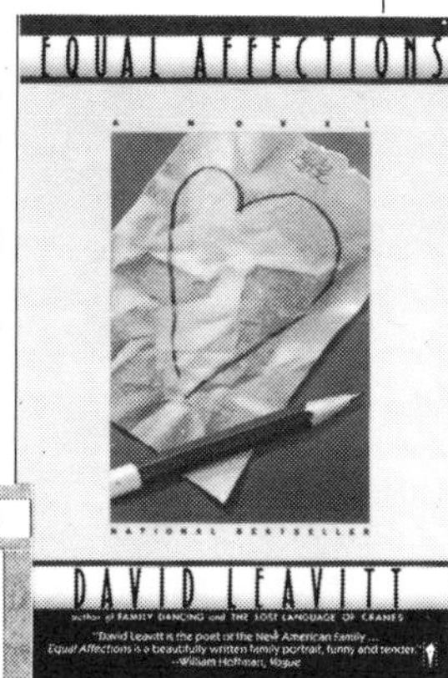

"Colwin writes with such sunny skill, and such tireless enthusiasm . . . one reads with fascination the steps by which lovers in one story after another stumble upon their forthright declarations."
—*New York Times Book Review.*
$7.95

"A rewarding expedition through the back alleys and main streets of a great city and the hearts of its irrepressible citizens."
—*San Francisco Chronicle.*
$8.95

"This fine collection . . . of nine lean, tough tales . . . offers a welcome introduction to a distinctive, original new voice in fiction."—*Cleveland Plain Dealer.* "I'm wild for it; I wish it were three times as long."
—Edward Hoagland.
$7.95

PERENNIAL LIBRARY
HARPER & ROW PUBLISHERS
Available in Canada from Harper & Collins

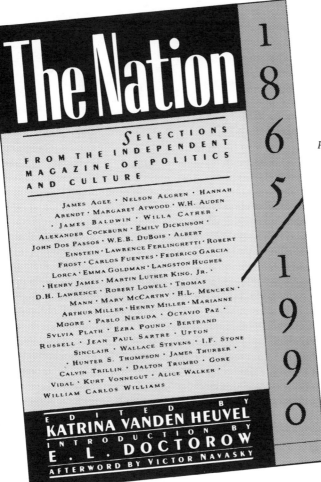

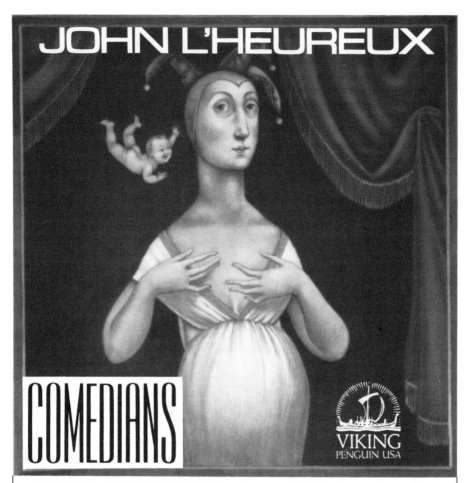

World of Literature

The House of Childhood

By Marie Luise Kaschnitz
Translated by Anni Whissen

Almost against her will, the narrator seeks out the House of Childhood, a sort of museum equipped with films and other media designed to help individuals recollect their early years. She confronts past events that her mind has suppressed and becomes painfully aware of her long-standing phobias and feelings of inadequacy and estrangement. *Das Haus der Kindheit* was first published in Germany in 1956. A volume in our series, European Women Writers. Available in December.
$23.95 cl, $8.95 pa

Bitter Healing

German Women Writers from 1700 to 1830, An Anthology

By Jeannine Blackwell and Susanne Zantop

Bitter Healing is the first anthology of eighteenth- and early nineteenth-century German women's writing in English translation. It goes far toward filling a major gap in literary history by recovering for a wide audience the works of women who were as famous during their lifetimes as Wieland, Schiller, and Goethe. A volume in our series, European Women Writers.
$38.50 cl, $14.95 pa

Winged Words

American Indian Writers Speak

By Laura Coltelli

Some of the most highly regarded contemporary Indian poets and novelists appear together for the first time in a book that illustrates the power of language. Laura Coltelli has interviewed Paula Gunn Allen, Michael Dorris, Louise Erdrich, Joy Harjo, Linda Hogan, N. Scott Momaday, Simon Ortiz, Wendy Rose, Leslie Marmon Silko, Gerald Vizenor, and James Welch. They candidly discuss major issues confronting American Indian writers today. A volume in our series, American Indian Lives. $22.50

ALGONQUIN BOOKS OF CHAPEL HILL

Volume I, Number I

THE VIEW FROM ALGONQUIN

Short musings on books, authors, and publishing, prepared from time to time by Algonquin Books of Chapel Hill

On "regional publishing," local talent... and literature that transcends geography

We were pleased to accept, some time back, a citation from the Ernest Hemingway Foundation for Kaye Gibbons' first novel, *Ellen Foster*—but were slightly bemused by the language:

> "In honoring *Ellen Foster*, we also pay tribute to the small regional presses now flourishing throughout this country..."

Not to seem ungrateful, and we do appreciate the kind words, but—Algonquin may be small, but we are not a regional press any more than Random House or Doubleday are regional presses because they are located in New York City.

The idea that our books are written for people in a specific area is absurd. Take Mississippian Larry Brown's new novel, *Dirty Work*, for example. Written fifty years after Dalton Trumbo's famous antiwar novel *Johnny Got His Gun*, *Dirty Work* bears comparison on many levels, for the same issues are at stake: war and peace, life and death, love. And while Brown's approach is as different from Trumbo's as the eighties are from the thirties, his novel achieves the same kind of universal power, delivers the same shocking recognition of human loss. What, then, is so all-fired "regional" about that?

Having said all that, it occurs to us that we *do* publish more than our share of outstanding Southern writers, especially in *New Stories from the South*.

The Algonquin Literary Quiz

Identify the sport played by the following fictional characters, and the book in which each appears: (a) Rabbit Angstrom; (b) The Citizen; (c) Labove; (d) Jordan Baker. *Answers, inverted, at bottom of page.*

Uncle Maxwell's Publishing Clinic

Uncle Maxwell will endeavor to answer your questions about publishing and related subjects.

Q. *Why do books cost so much these days? Several decades ago, books cost $3, $4, and $5. You'd think that with computerized typesetting and photoprinting, books could be printed more economically. It is getting so that I cannot afford to buy anything but paperback books.*

—N.L., New York, NY

A. The envelope in which you enclosed your letter has a 25¢ postage stamp on it. Back in the Good Old Days, the same letter would have taken a 3¢ stamp. Does that answer your question?

TO BE CONTINUED...

Address correspondence, if any, to Algonquin Books of Chapel Hill, Post Office Box 2225, Chapel Hill, N.C. 27515-2225

(a) Basketball, Updike, *Rabbit, Run*; (b) Shotput, Joyce, *Ulysses*; (c) Football, Faulkner, *The Hamlet*; (d) Golf, Fitzgerald, *The Great Gatsby*.

ALGONQUIN BOOKS OF CHAPEL HILL

The Poetry Center of the 92nd Street Y

Calendar of Readings 1990-91

September	17	**William Styron** reads from his memoir *Darkness Visible*
	23	**Wallace Stegner** and **David Leavitt**
	25	**Writers-at-Work Live Interview:** **Donald Hall** is interviewed by **Peter Stitt**
	25	**Donald Hall** and **Frank Bidart** read from their work
October	8	MEXICAN LITERATURE FESTIVAL **Octavio Paz** is interviewed by **Alfred MacAdam**
	8	**Octavio Paz** reads from his work
	15	Fiction writer **Elena Poniatowska** and poet **José Emilio Pacheco**
	22	**Josephine Jacobsen** and **Anne Winters**
	29	**John Edgar Wideman** and **Terry McMillan**
November	5	**Claire Bloom: An Evening of Poetry and Music**
	12	**GEOGRAPHIES I: Barry Lopez** reads from his work
	19	**Writers-at-Work Live Interview:** **Reynolds Price** is interviewed by **Frederick Busch**
	19	**Reynolds Price** reads from his work
	26	**Don DeLillo** and **Paul Auster**
December	3	**POETS AND PAINTERS:** **John Ashbery, Jane Freilicher, Kenneth Koch, Larry Rivers**
	10	**Robert Creeley, Brice Marden, Jorie Graham, Eric Fischl**
	17	**John Hollander, Wayne Thiebaud, Mark Strand, William Bailey**
January	14	**John Barth** and **John Hawkes**
	21	**August Wilson**
	28	WRITERS ON NEW YORK: **Joyce Johnson, Alfred Kazin** and **Phillip Lopate**
February	4	**Doris Lessing**
	11	**The Tenth Muse I: Amy Clampitt** introduces **Julia Budenz, Melissa Green** and **Kathleen Norris**
	25	**Norman Mailer** reads from his new novel
March	4	**Robert Hass** and **Daniel Halpern**
	11	**Amos Oz**, Israel novelist and essayist
	18	**Hayden Carruth** and **Lynne Sharon Schwartz**
	25	**The Tenth Muse II: Galway Kinnell** introduces **Carol Conroy, Toi Derricotte and Li-Young Lee**
April	1	**GEOGRAPHIES II: Rick Bass** and **Gretel Erhlich**
	8	**Philip Levine** and **Linda Bierds**
	15	**Elizabeth Spencer** and **Kaye Gibbons**
	22	**Writers-at-Work Live Interview:** **Denise Levertov** is interviewed by **Deborah Digges**
	22	**Denise Levertov** and **Christopher Gilbert** read from their work
	29	**"Discovery"/*The Nation* 1991 Poetry Contest Winners**
May	6	**Abraham Sutzkever,** Preeminent Yiddish poet
	13	**Bobbie Ann Mason** and **Jane Smiley**
	21	**E.L. Doctorow**

For more information about The Poetry Center's workshops and reading series, please call (212) 415-5760. To charge tickets call (212) 996-1100.
The 92nd Street Y. 1395 Lexington Ave., NYC 10128 An agency of UJA-Federation.